ARMOR UP
study

Armor Up—Copyright ©2023 by Amber Olafsson & Dianne Wyper
Published by UNITED HOUSE Publishing

All rights reserved. No portion of this book may be reproduced or shared in any form—electronic, printed, photocopied, recording, or by any information storage and retrieval system, without prior written permission from the publisher. The use of short quotations is permitted.

Scriptures marked (ESV) are from The ESV® Bible (The Holy Bible, English Standard Version®), copyright © 2001 by Crossway, a publishing ministry of Good News Publishers. Used by permission. All rights reserved.

Scriptures marked (NIV) are from THE HOLY BIBLE, NEW INTERNATIONAL VERSION® NIV® Copyright © 1973, 1978, 1984 by International Bible Society® Used by permission. All rights reserved worldwide.

Scripture marked (KJV) are taken from The Authorized (King James) Version. Rights in the Authorized Version in the United Kingdom are vested in the Crown. Reproduced by permission of the Crown's patentee, Cambridge University Press

Scripture marked (NLT) are taken from the Holy Bible, New Living Translation, copyright © 1996, 2004, 2015 by Tyndale House Foundation. Used by permission of Tyndale House Publishers, Inc., Carol Stream, Illinois 60188. All rights reserved.

Scripture marked (BSB) are taken from The Holy Bible, Berean Study Bible, BSB Copyright ©2016, 2020 by Bible Hub Used by Permission. All Rights Reserved Worldwide.
https://bereanbible.com

Scripture taken from the New King James Version®. Copyright © 1982 by Thomas Nelson. Used by permission. All rights reserved.

Scripture quotations taken from the (NASB®) New American Standard Bible®, Copyright © 1960, 1971, 1977, 1995, 2020 by The Lockman Foundation. Used by permission. All rights reserved. lockman.org"

Scripture quotations marked (AMP) are taken from the Amplified Bible, Copyright © 2015 by The Lockman Foundation. Used by permission.

ISBN-978-1-952840-40-1

UNITED HOUSE Publishing
Waterford, Michigan
info@unitedhousepublishing.com
www.unitedhousepublishing.com

Cover and interior design: Amber Olafsson, Dianne Wyper, and Nevaeh Wyper
Author photography: Drew Olafsson, Meg Lince, megolincephotography.com

Printed in the United States of America
2023—First Edition

SPECIAL SALES
Most UNITED HOUSE books are available at special quantity discounts when purchased in bulk by corporations, organizations, and special-interest groups. For information, please e-mail orders@unitedhousepublishing.com

*To our families, we are grateful God chose us to engage in warfare together.
We could not war or have written this book on God's armor without you.
You are mighty warriors in the Lord and we are thankful for your sacrifice.*

SCAN HERE TO
WATCH THE
WEEKLY
ARMOR UP
VIDEOS

REASON FOR STARTING

_____

DATE STARTED

_____

WE ENCOURAGE YOU TO MAKE A COMMITMENT TO FINISH THIS STUDY IN THE NEXT 40 DAYS. CONSIDER THIS YOUR SPIRITUAL BOOT CAMP TO EQUIP YOU IN BECOMING ALL THAT GOD HAS CREATED YOU TO BE!

FINISH DATE

_____

Put on the full armor of God

Armor Up

CONTENTS

INTRODUCTION	2
The Armor of God	5
Belt of Truth	27
Breastplate of Righteousness	49
The Cornerstone	79
The Plumb Line	105
Robe of Royalty	129
Shoes of the Gospel of Peace	153
Helmet of Salvation	178
Sword of the Spirit	203
Shield of Faith	233
FINAL WORD	258

GET THE MOST FROM THIS STUDY

There are many 'Armor of God' studies, what makes this one unique? This entire Bible study was birthed while we read through the Old Testament book of Zechariah. Flipping through the pages of the ancient account of the rebuilding of God's physical temple in Jerusalem, we started noticing something: pieces of the armor of God, hidden amongst Old Testament history. Since we, the followers of Jesus, are the spiritual temple of God in the New Testament, we begin to find parallels between Zechariah's story of building the Old Testament temple, and Paul's description of the Armor of God for us, the New Testament temple. Check out the parallels on the next few pages.

HELPFUL TIP

Utilize www.biblehub.com, both to dig deeper into the Hebrew and Greek meanings of words, but also when filling in the blanks throughout the study. This is an easy resource which allows you to look at multiple translations at one time.

BELT OF TRUTH	BREASTPLATE OF RIGHTEOUSNESS	SHOES FITTED WITH THE GOSPEL OF PEACE
But this is what you must do: Tell the <u>truth</u> to each other. Render verdicts in your courts that are just and that lead to peace. Zechariah 8:16 NLT Love <u>truth</u> and peace. Zechariah 8:19b NLT	Do not despise these small beginnings, for the LORD rejoices to see the work begin, to see the <u>plumb line</u> in Zerubbabel's hand. Zechariah 4:10 NLT (We realize this might not make sense right now, but it will!) I will bring them to dwell in the midst of Jerusalem. And they shall be my people, and I will be their God, in faithfulness and in <u>righteousness</u>. Zechariah 8:8 ESV	For I am planting seeds of <u>peace</u> and prosperity among you. Zechariah 8:12 NLT But this is what you must do: Tell the truth to each other. Render verdicts in your courts that are just and that lead to <u>peace</u>. Zechariah 8:16 NLT Love truth and <u>peace</u>. Zechariah 8:19b NLT

Armor Up

HELMET OF SALVATION	SWORD OF THE SPIRIT	SHEILD OF FAITH
And the LORD will give <u>salvation</u> to the tents of Judah first, that the glory of the house of David and the glory of the inhabitants of Jerusalem may not surpass that of Judah. Zechariah 12:7 ESV The LORD their God will <u>save</u> his people on that day as a shepherd saves his flock. They will sparkle in his land like jewels in a crown. Zechariah 9:16 NIV	So he said to me, "This is the word of the LORD to Zerubbabel: 'Not by might nor by power, but by my <u>Spirit</u>,' says the LORD Almighty. Zechariah 4:6 NIV	On that day the LORD will <u>shield</u> those who live in Jerusalem, so that the feeblest among them will be like David, and the house of David will be like God, like the angel of the LORD going before them. Zechariah 12:8 NIV I will bring them to dwell in the midst of Jerusalem. And they shall be my people, and I will be their God, in <u>faithfulness</u> and in righteousness. Zechariah 8:8 ESV

INTRODUCTION

The battle is on. Tensions are high. The army of darkness and light are constantly warring for the win, and all the chaos can make us want to stay home and just pray for Jesus to return and get us out of this world. But what if hiding and hoping it all just goes away isn't what God wants us to do? What if when Jesus ascended and sent down His Holy Spirit, He wanted to not only comfort and help us, but clothe us with His power and authority to take back ground the enemy has stolen? In this study, we're going to learn how to wear the 'armor of light' and see victory in every area of our life and out in the world. It's time to shine, radiant warrior, and dethrone the darkness—Jesus has already done it, we just need to learn to apply His victory and walk it out.

We hope that throughout this study you will be encouraged, challenged, and built by truths found in the Word of God. Our prayer is that the Holy Spirit works through every session as we process, talk through, and soak in all the Lord wants to reveal. This study is an invitation to Armor Up. It's a challenge to take a deep dive into Ephesians six and really grasp what it means to put on the armor of God. Although this armor in scripture is depicted as a harsh, heavy covering for intense battle, we think you'll be surprised at what armoring up actually looks like.

Be ready, because this armor we're talking about is more than just a collection of military gear, it's actually a way of life and if worn correctly, will change the game, much to the enemy's dismay. He will no longer have the access that he may currently have. We believe your response to warfare is about to change forever and will more than likely take a drastic shift—and in the midst of it all you can experience absolute peace. You might be thinking: **Wait, I thought you were talking about war?** Yeah, but we've discovered the secret of peace that can only be found when you truly understand what God's armor really is. We can't wait for you to see it all come together. Are you ready to Armor Up? Come on, let's dive in!

THE ARMOR OF GOD
week one

Be strong in the Lord and in His mighty power. Put on the full armor of God so that you can take your stand against the devil's schemes.

EPHESIANS 6:10-11

Stepping out onto the battlefield, the professionally trained soldiers couldn't believe their eyes—surely this young boy was ill-equipped to face a giant twice his size. With no armor and no weapons of war, what could he do? The armies of Israel needed a savior, not a kid.

Though the atmosphere was filled with skepticism, young David was full of confidence . . . in His God. Driven by purpose and brimming with courage the ruddy young man marched across the Valley of Elah in assurance. While the stones in his shepherd's pouch rattled with each step, his nerves did not.

Even though King Saul offered his armor, David knew his real protection came from the Lord and His promises—the unfamiliar armor was both uncomfortable and unhelpful. As he approached the evil foe Goliath, the enemy smirked and prematurely celebrated his anticipated victory over a seemingly unprepared, weak adversary. But David didn't skip a beat, unfazed at the threats and laughs of the enemy, because he knew something Goliath did not: looks can be deceiving. David knew who he was, knew he was trained, and knew what His God could do. Sliding one smooth stone into his shepherd's sling and swinging it with all his might, he attacked and swiftly defeated the giant, becoming a legend. Wearing not the armor of men, but the armor of God—clothed in His promises and protection—he did the impossible. Eventually David became the greatest warrior and king Israel ever had.

Saul had one set of armor and David had another. Saul's was visible, heavy, and ill-fitting. David's was invisible, light, and relied on the strength and promises of God. Saul thought his man-made armor would provide protection, but David knew God was his only safeguard. In the same way, when we put on the wrong, man-made armor we struggle to defeat our enemy, but when we are clothed in the armor of God, we'll see the victory.

So what is this invisible armor of God? Ephesians six may be very familiar to you, but perhaps you haven't heard it described this way. This week we're diving a little deeper and uncovering other places in the Bible God's armor is mentioned to get a clearer picture.

THE ARMOR OF GOD

Scan for session one video

SESSION ONE NOTES:

DAY ONE
be strong in the Lord

God is looking to raise an army, but before we take one step on the battlefield we need to Armor Up—wearing the correct protection. Our study is based on the armor of God listed in Ephesians six, but if you've been in church any amount of time we're guessing you've already done a study or heard a sermon on this passage . . . but not like this. Imagine you've never read this passage before. Ask the Holy Spirit to reveal something you've never seen in these familiar Bible verses and let's see what He illuminates.

Say a quick prayer for fresh eyes and an open, teachable heart and turn in the Bible or look up on Biblehub.com Ephesians chapter six. Read it outloud and see if anything new jumps out at you? Next, fill in the words:

> FINALLY, BE STRONG IN THE _____ AND IN HIS MIGHTY POWER. PUT ON THE _____, SO THAT YOU CAN TAKE YOUR _____ AGAINST THE DEVIL'S SCHEMES. FOR OUR STRUGGLE IS NOT AGAINST _____, BUT AGAINST THE RULERS, AGAINST THE AUTHORITIES, AGAINST THE POWERS OF THIS DARK WORLD AND AGAINST THE _____ IN THE HEAVENLY REALMS. THEREFORE _____ THE FULL ARMOR OF GOD, SO THAT WHEN THE DAY OF EVIL COMES, YOU MAY BE ABLE TO _____, AND AFTER YOU HAVE DONE EVERYTHING, TO STAND.
> EPHESIANS 6:10-13 NIV

Reading through this passage, was anything highlighted to you? Share why this hit you in a different way.

Do you consider yourself "strong in the Lord"? Why or why not?

Notice the phrase "put on"? We thought it would be helpful to look at the Greek definition of this to give us more insight. Look at this!

The Greek word for "put on" is *enduo*: I put on, clothe, be clothed with (in the sense of sinking into a garment) [1]

RESEARCH MORE

Sinking into a garment? Now we don't know about you, but we have never thought of "sinking into" the armor of God. There is something peaceful about this definition. But did you notice when you put on the full armor of God then you CAN take a stand against the enemy? We believe throughout this study as we let these truths sink into us, we will truly be clothed in the FULL armor of God and be positioned to take our stand against the devil's schemes; and not only stand but live a victorious life.

Paul declares our struggle is not against who?

Do you tend to see people as your enemy or the lie, ideology, or spirit behind their actions/words?

Right now is there a person you consider an adversary? How can you release them from this label?

As we embark on this *Armor Up* journey, let's keep that visual of sinking into the armor of God before us. Let's make it our aim to use this study to strengthen us in the LORD, and remember who the real enemy is.

SECRET PLACE Training

When we harbor unforgiveness, it can prevent what God wants to do in our lives. At the onset of this study, we want to empty ourselves of anything heavy or ill-fitting. You see, when we are wounded or we've gone down the wrong path, we often put up walls or defense mechanisms to protect us, but this is like wearing Saul's ill-fitting and unhelpful armor. It doesn't bring us victory or true protection, it locks us up.

COUNT UP THE DEBT

We're going to do an activity to count up the debt and remove it. Ask the Lord to remind you of anything you have not healed from: this includes things done to or words spoken over you, and even things you have done. Count up the debt. Total it ALL up. Spend time in the presence of the Lord and say:

FATHER, IT WAS WRONG WHEN _____, DID THIS TO ME . . .

WHEN THIS PERSON SAID _____, IT HURT ME LORD . . .

IT WAS WRONG WHEN I DID _____, I'M SORRY LORD . . .

Once you've thought of everything, surrender it to Jesus. Give these people, their actions, and even your mistakes into the hands of your Savior. Close your eyes and picture you surrendering the record of debt to Jesus. What does He do with it? Did He nail it to the cross? Does he burn it? Does He put it under his feet? Now release the hurts, sins, and offenses to the Lord. Ask Him to help you forgive others.

Ephesians six armor of God description begins with, "Be strong in the Lord." It doesn't say you have to muster up your own strength to forgive, but the strength to do this comes from the Lord. He will help. Receive His forgiveness that He released to you thousands of years ago on the cross. Forgive others and yourself. He has.

Journaling

DAY TWO
learning to rest in Jesus

Soooo the armor of God is something Christians are ALREADY wearing?! YEAH. But perhaps not utilizing? ALSO CORRECT. Many of us think the armor of God is something we need to wake up and put on every day, like an invisible military uniform, but really the armor is Jesus, it is His covering. Every believer is covered in Christ, but do we know what that means? How does this apply to us practically? In this study, we're unpacking truths about Him—what He did for us and who we are in Him—it is a reminder to see ourselves clothed in Christ. We are armed for war when we realize we are hidden in Christ forever. Over the next few weeks, we'll unpack each piece and reveal how it points to Christ. He is actually our defense and weapon. Let's look at some of the points from the introduction video and dig into even more scriptures. We can really sum up the whole study with:

Wearing the armor of God is really just resting in Jesus.

Does God want us to rest in Jesus? What does the Word say?

Look up the scripture and fill in the blanks below:

> THEREFORE, SINCE THE PROMISE OF ENTERING HIS _____ STILL STANDS, LET US BE CAREFUL THAT NONE OF YOU BE FOUND TO HAVE FALLEN SHORT OF IT. FOR WE ALSO HAVE HAD THE _____ PROCLAIMED TO US, JUST AS THEY DID; BUT THE MESSAGE THEY HEARD WAS OF NO VALUE TO THEM, BECAUSE THEY DID NOT SHARE THE _____ OF THOSE WHO OBEYED . . . FOR ANYONE WHO ENTERS GOD'S _____ ALSO RESTS FROM THEIR WORKS, JUST AS GOD DID FROM HIS.
> HEBREWS 4:1-2 & 10 NIV

God has a rest planned for His people, a rest from "their works." We enter this rest when we hear the message of "the good news"—which is the Gospel of Jesus Christ—and believe it by faith.

The writer of Hebrews is trying to tell us we can rest in the "good news"—which is what Jesus did. We know that Jesus wants us to experience this rest because of what He says He will give to those who come to Him. Finish the following sentence:

> "COME TO ME, ALL YOU WHO ARE WEARY AND BURDENED, AND I WILL GIVE YOU _____"
> MATTHEW 11:28 NIV.

God wants us to rest in our identity in Christ, and the enemy wants us to always question whether we are hidden in Jesus. Wearing the armor is a constant awareness that we're forever found in Christ. God will never look at believers without the covering of Jesus. Can I get an AMEN?!

Colossians 3:3 says our life is . . . ?

How do you view yourself? Do you see yourself as hidden in Christ, or do you see yourself outside of Christ? How do you think God sees you?

Colossians 3:3 declares "we died" and our life is now hidden and unified with Jesus.

Let's skip over a few verses to Colossians 3:10. What are we supposed to "put on"?

This is the same word used in the armor of God . . . the Lord wants us to "sink into" the truth that we have been gifted a new nature, one that is created to be just like God. Which means each day we should be less like our old selves and be more like Jesus. When we focus on the fact that we are clothed in Christ, then we start walking in His ways. What we behold is what we become.

It's evident that the armor of God is your new identity in Christ. Start beholding that!

SECRET PLACE Training

Today, the focus is truly resting in Jesus. As you sit alone with the Lord ask Him: *Am I resting in who I am in You, or am I constantly striving to work for something that has already been gifted to me?* Write down what He reveals:

Journaling

Journaling

In the Old Testament book of Zechariah, a man named Joshua, who was the high priest, was being attacked by the enemy. At first, Joshua was wearing filthy rags. Read Zechariah 3:1-4 and let the Lord speak to you about how He sees you and what He thinks of the enemy's constant accusations against you. How does this encourage you to know that God has clothed you in the perfection of Jesus, and gifted you a new nature?

Ask yourself:

Do I see myself forgiven and clothed in Jesus, or do I see the filthy rags of sin and my old nature, continually recounting what I've done wrong?

DAY THREE
the armor is Jesus

WHY have we never seen this before?! Y'all we had an epiphany while studying the pieces of armor listed in Ephesians six! Each piece in some way described Jesus and the gospel. Have you ever viewed the armor this way? Let's do a quick summary of each piece of armor and see where in the Word this lines up with a truth about Christ. Look up the scriptures and fill in the blanks.

BELT OF TRUTH

JESUS ANSWERED, 'I AM THE WAY AND THE _____ AND THE LIFE. NO ONE COMES TO THE FATHER EXCEPT THROUGH ME.'
JOHN 14:6 NIV

BREASTPLATE OF RIGHTEOUSNESS

IT IS BECAUSE OF HIM THAT YOU ARE IN CHRIST JESUS, WHO HAS BECOME FOR US WISDOM FROM . . . GOD—THAT IS, OUR _____, HOLINESS AND REDEMPTION."
1 CORINTHIANS 1:30 NIV

"AND THIS WILL BE HIS NAME: 'THE LORD IS OUR _____.' IN THAT DAY JUDAH WILL BE SAVED, AND ISRAEL WILL LIVE IN SAFETY."
JEREMIAH 23:6 NLT

SHIELD OF FAITH

. . . LOOKING TO JESUS, THE FOUNDER AND PERFECTER OF OUR _____, WHO FOR THE JOY THAT WAS SET BEFORE HIM ENDURED THE CROSS, DESPISING THE SHAME, AND IS SEATED AT THE RIGHT HAND OF THE THRONE OF GOD.
HEBREWS 12:2 ESV

HELMET OF SALVATION

JESUS IS 'THE STONE YOU BUILDERS REJECTED, WHICH HAS BECOME THE CORNERSTONE.' _____ IS FOUND IN NO ONE ELSE, FOR THERE IS NO OTHER NAME UNDER HEAVEN GIVEN TO MANKIND BY WHICH WE MUST BE _____ .
ACTS 4:11-12 NIV

THE LORD LIVES! BLESSED BE MY ROCK! LET GOD BE EXALTED, THE ROCK OF MY _____ ! 2 SAMUEL 22:47 NKJV

SWORD OF THE SPIRIT

IN HIS RIGHT HAND HE HELD SEVEN STARS, AND COMING OUT OF HIS MOUTH WAS A SHARP, DOUBLE-EDGED _____ . HIS FACE WAS LIKE THE SUN SHINING IN ALL ITS BRILLIANCE.
REVELATION 1:16 NIV

YOU, HOWEVER, ARE NOT IN THE FLESH BUT IN THE SPIRIT, IF IN FACT THE SPIRIT OF GOD DWELLS IN YOU. ANYONE WHO DOES NOT HAVE THE SPIRIT OF _____ DOES NOT BELONG TO HIM. ROMANS 8:9 ESV

SHOES FIT WITH THE GOSPEL OF PEACE

BUT NOW IN CHRIST JESUS YOU WHO ONCE WERE FAR AWAY HAVE BEEN BROUGHT NEAR BY THE BLOOD OF CHRIST. FOR HE HIMSELF IS OUR _____ . . .
EPHESIANS 2:13-14 NIV

Did y'all have any lightbulbs go off while reading through these scriptures?

Which piece of the armor and its connection to Jesus stood out the most to you? Why?

SECRET PLACE *Training*

Spend some time with the Lord today and ask Him to teach you a deeper meaning of the armor of God. Inquire of Him, *Is the armor really describing Jesus? Teach and guide me Lord. Show me more verses that confirm this.*

journal

Today's challenge is to find more scriptures throughout the Bible that line up the character and attributes of Jesus to the pieces of the armor.

Example: Where else is Jesus and peace connected? What more can you find about our righteousness being tied to Christ? Write down a few verses you find!

journal

DAY FOUR
the armor throughout the Bible

Apparently the armor of God isn't only mentioned in Ephesians six! WHAT?! Who knew? Let's look through other places in the Bible where this Heavenly armor is mentioned to gain even more understanding about what we're clothed in. Look up the following scriptures and fill in the blanks:

Romans

THE NIGHT IS NEARLY OVER; THE DAY IS ALMOST HERE. SO LET US PUT ASIDE THE DEEDS OF DARKNESS AND PUT ON THE ARMOR OF_____.
LET US BEHAVE DECENTLY, AS IN THE DAYTIME, NOT IN CAROUSING AND DRUNKENNESS, NOT IN SEXUAL IMMORALITY AND DEBAUCHERY, NOT IN DISSENSION AND JEALOUSY. RATHER, _____ YOURSELVES WITH THE LORD _____, AND DO NOT THINK ABOUT HOW TO GRATIFY THE DESIRES OF THE FLESH.
ROMANS 13:12-14 NIV

What is the armor called here?

The end of this passage tells us what wearing the armor really means. What does it say: "Rather be clothed in" who?

The armor is Jesus. And when we're clothed in Him, did you notice what we won't gratify? The desires of the flesh. We must understand, as believers, we have been clothed in Jesus, this is how we overcome! Understanding our identity, knowing we are now one with Him and have been made new!

Thessalonians

BUT SINCE WE BELONG
TO THE DAY, LET
US BE SOBER, PUTTING ON FAITH AND _____ AS A BREASTPLATE, AND THE HOPE OF _____ AS
A HELMET.
THESSALONIANS 5:8 NIV

What other attribute to the armor did Paul mention here?

Armor Up

Love seems like it would be this fluffy, not real powerful addition to the battle gear . . . but 2 Timothy 1:7 begs to differ.

*For God has not given us a spirit of fear, but of **power** and of **love** and of a **sound mind**.* NKJV

Fear is a formidable foe, but God sent a solution . . . His Spirit which is full of: power and love. You see love, power, and a sound mind are all connected. Love is power. Love actually casts out fear (see 1 John 4:8). Love guards our hearts and minds against bitterness and fills us with compassion. Love is so strong; it is what motivated the Father to send Jesus to rescue us.

Did you notice that "anger" is not a part of the armor of God, but love is? Anger also isn't a fruit of the Spirit listed in Galatians 5 — this fruit is evidence of His activity in our lives. We don't know about y'all but we're thinking if we are going off to war, it seems like anger would be a better asset than love. However, we believe this is on purpose because God doesn't want us warring from a place of anger, but love.

He sent Jesus to the biggest showdown of darkness vs. light ever because of love—His love for humanity not hatred and disgust (1 John 4:9). Check out what the following verses have to say on the subject.

> WHOEVER IS SLOW TO _____ IS BETTER THAN THE MIGHTY, AND HE WHO RULES HIS SPIRIT THAN HE WHO TAKES A CITY. PROVERBS 16:32 ESV

> KNOW THIS, MY BELOVED BROTHERS: LET EVERY PERSON BE QUICK TO HEAR, SLOW TO SPEAK, SLOW TO _____; FOR THE _____ OF MAN DOES NOT PRODUCE THE RIGHTEOUSNESS OF GOD. JAMES 1:19-20 ESV

See how man's anger doesn't lead people to righteousness? We are in a battle to win souls for the Kingdom. As brothers and sisters, we need to be careful we aren't breaking the bond between God and the world with our anger because He's trying to win them back with truth and love. When we minister out of anger we push people away from God, not draw them closer. Let's live out Romans 2:4 which declares it's the kindness of God that leads people to repent.

Jesus *did not* say we will be known by our "righteous anger", but what *did* He say would be the proof we follow Him?_____

By this all people will know that you are my disciples, if you have _____ *for one another.* John 13:35 ESV

We're taking back society and culture, our family, city, country, and world not because we're full of anger, but full of love for these beautiful gifts God has given us. Oh, love is a needed element of the armor, a mighty defender and conqueror indeed!

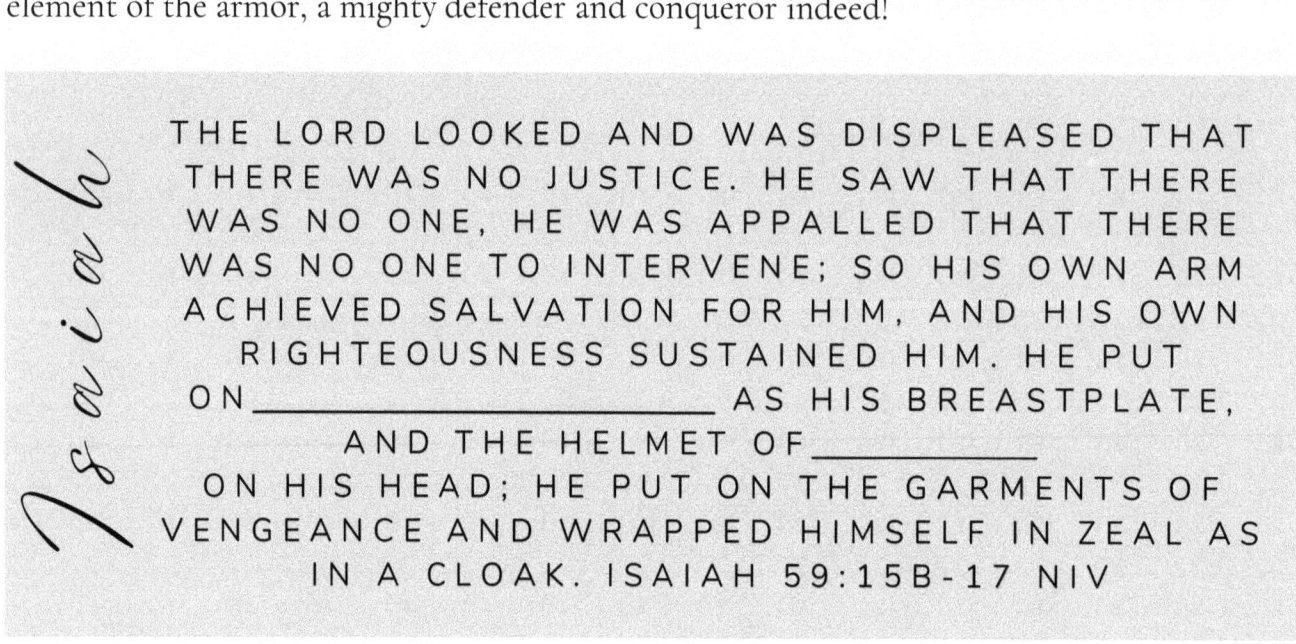

THE LORD LOOKED AND WAS DISPLEASED THAT THERE WAS NO JUSTICE. HE SAW THAT THERE WAS NO ONE, HE WAS APPALLED THAT THERE WAS NO ONE TO INTERVENE; SO HIS OWN ARM ACHIEVED SALVATION FOR HIM, AND HIS OWN RIGHTEOUSNESS SUSTAINED HIM. HE PUT ON_____ AS HIS BREASTPLATE, AND THE HELMET OF_____ ON HIS HEAD; HE PUT ON THE GARMENTS OF VENGEANCE AND WRAPPED HIMSELF IN ZEAL AS IN A CLOAK. ISAIAH 59:15B-17 NIV

We love how this passage describes the very armor Jesus wore when He came to the earth to intervene for humanity and bring justice through the cross. He was clothed in the armor of God y'all, that is how He overcame the world. The beautiful thing is: He gifted us this mighty protection to wear as well! It's Him! It's His very own covering!

Wrapping up this week, we wanted to just reiterate: our covering is Jesus and His work on the cross. Sometimes we can be tempted to believe our own works are our covering . . . perhaps thinking, as long as we've crossed our t's and dotted our i's—as long as we've followed the rules enough—then we are covered. But the covering and protection has never been based on us, but based on what Jesus has done for us. HE ALONE IS OUR COVERING. His work at the cross was enough. It's time to believe it and stand in the armor of light. The light of the gospel! This is such good news!!!

SECRET PLACE Training

As you spend time with the Lord today ask:

- Am I truly clothed in Christ or am I clothed in self?
- Do I pay more attention to what I do for You, than what You did for me?
- Am I wearing love or anger?

Father, reveal any areas I need to trust in Your protection, and help me walk in Your armor. Help me believe as a Christian I am clothed in Christ! Give me Heaven's perspective! Remind me: When You look at me, You see your Son. I trust in Jesus and what He did for me! I am hidden in Christ!

Journaling

BELT OF TRUTH
week two

Stand firm then with the belt of truth buckled around your waist.

EPHESIANS 6:14

Is it Wednesday yet?! ATTENDING A MOM'S GROUP in my early years of mothering was a godsend. Wednesday was a morning of relaxation and connection I looked forward to every week. I was able to drop off my kids in a sweet little class where they were taught about Jesus and played with other children their age, and the moms got to have a breather, drink a cup of coffee, be poured into, and interact with other adults. A win-win for all involved. It was a glorious, needed, weekly refreshment.

One week we were super tight on money, as in our account was at zero. The gas tank in my car was empty, we were out of groceries, and my husband was not getting paid until the following day. All these factors added up to a discouraged mama, who wasn't going to be able to attend my weekly group to be refreshed. I was upset, feeling poor, and eating sautéed corn for a snack because that is all I could find. I am not even joking. Did I mention I was hungry? (Or hangry. However you want to look at it.) And that always makes every circumstance WAY worse than it actually is. *Can I get an amen?* My tear-filled eyes were completely focused on my situation, and it looked bleak. All I could see was lack.

Then a familiar Bible verse came to me, "And God shall supply for your needs according to His riches in glory." (Phil 4:19)

As I pondered the facts of my circumstance and the truth of Scripture, I had a choice to make. Would I trust His Word and believe in a greater supernatural reality, or would I stay fixed on what I could see in the natural and wallow in self-pity? Do I believe in what I see or what He said, was the question of the hour?

I chose to put the spotlight on God and His promise. And in that moment, when my gaze shifted from problem to solution I declared: "God, I trust you. I believe your Word is the truth—regardless of what I see—and you are going to meet my need—you always have, and you always will."

As the words left my lips, instantly an unexplainable peace washed over me. Ten minutes later I got a phone call from my . . .

husband, "Hey, you are never going to guess what happened! We just got paid a day early. I'm heading to the bank!" (*Come on, Jesus!!*) That had NEVER happened before.

Overcome with thankfulness, I cried tears of joy and relief. The LORD showed me He could be trusted and the importance of keeping my focus on the correct thing that day: the truth of God's Word. This was a lesson I'll never forget . . . facts aren't truth. What God says is the truth, period. I've learned when the circumstances don't align with scripture, I have an opportunity to declare God's Word over the situation and command it to come into alignment with His Kingdom reality. What we see and what the Bible says are often two different things. But at the end of the day, we put on the 'belt of truth' when we learn to walk by "faith" in what God has said, despite what we see. Not only do we believe in a greater supernatural truth, but we declare it, and it's a game changer.

— Amber

THE BELT OF TRUTH

Scan for session two video

SESSION TWO NOTES:

DAY ONE
Jesus is the Word

Therefore, put on every piece of God's armor so you will be able to resist the enemy in the time of evil. Then after the battle you will still be standing firm. Stand your ground, putting on the belt of truth . . . **Ephesians 6:13-14a NLT**

Today, let's unpack what it means to put on the belt of truth. First of all, what is truth? Well, Jesus makes it clear in scripture that He is the truth. Fill in the blank:

> JESUS ANSWERED, "I AM THE WAY AND THE _____ AND THE LIFE. NO ONE COMES TO THE FATHER EXCEPT THROUGH ME."
> JOHN 14:6 NIV

He is the way, He is the truth, and He is the life. Again, the belt of truth is ALL about Jesus.

The Bible also says that Jesus is the Word of God, fill in the blank (pay attention to capitalization):

> IN THE BEGINNING WAS THE _____ AND THE _____ WAS WITH GOD . . .

> AND THE _____ WAS GOD, THE _____ BECAME FLESH AND MADE HIS DWELLING AMONG US. WE HAVE SEEN HIS GLORY, THE GLORY OF THE ONE AND ONLY SON, WHO CAME FROM THE FATHER, FULL OF GRACE AND TRUTH.
> JOHN 1:1 & 14 NIV

Jesus is the Word and Jesus is the truth. So, clearly the belt of truth is being clothed in Christ and also, we believe being filled with the Word. This means taking time to read it, memorize, and let it change you.

Check out this description of Jesus from Revelation and pay close attention to what He is called and His name:

> I SAW HEAVEN STANDING OPEN AND THERE BEFORE ME WAS A WHITE HORSE, WHOSE RIDER IS CALLED FAITHFUL AND _____. WITH JUSTICE HE JUDGES AND WAGES WAR. HIS EYES ARE LIKE BLAZING FIRE . . .

> AND ON HIS HEAD ARE MANY CROWNS. HE HAS A NAME WRITTEN ON HIM THAT NO ONE KNOWS BUT HE HIMSELF. HE IS DRESSED IN A ROBE DIPPED IN BLOOD, AND HIS NAME IS THE _____.
> REVELATION 19:11-13 NIV

Guys, another name of Jesus is 'Word of God.' So, imagine now that every time you open up the Word you are opening up Jesus, you are literally spending time with Him! Truth is a powerful thing to wrap our hearts and minds around because there is power in the name of Jesus and the devil has to bow at his name. So, if the Word of God is actually one of the names of Jesus, then the enemy must bow at the declarations of Scripture too!! *Amen?!*

Do you get the power that we as Christ followers have been given, not only in the name of Jesus but also, in His Word?! What if we began to declare the Word of God over our circumstances, and situations? What if we started to prophesy the Word of God over people, places, and scenarios and watch God move in mighty miraculous ways? Friends, let's decide to learn, study, memorize, and speak the Scriptures like we never have before and begin to prophesy victories of truth while standing firm in faith on the cornerstone Jesus!

SECRET PLACE Training

We have the privilege of moving mountains with every Scripture that we declare in faith. What mountains are you facing right now? Ask the Lord to show you a greater supernatural reality in His Word to speak over this mountain. Is it financial? Relational? Sickness? God has promises for every single obstacle we face. Put on the belt of truth today by searching through the Bible and finding your promise to declare!

What am I up against?

What Bible verse speaks to this situation?

scriptures

Meditate on the Scriptures you find and let the power of God's word sink into your head and hearts!

Journaling

DAY TWO
the Spirit of truth

Not only do we have truth as we discussed yesterday both in Jesus and the Word of God, but we also have the Holy Spirit who is called the Spirit of truth (John 14:17). Why is He referred to as the Spirit of truth? Because He inspired the written Word of God. His job is to lead us into and help us understand all truth. It's the Holy Spirit that helps us know Jesus better and it's "by the Spirit that we cry Abba Father," therefore, through the Spirit we come to know the Father better too. This is so amazing, y'all! God actually gives us his Spirit to help us live in the fullness of His truth, His Word, and His Son. He's so good!

Look up these scriptures and fill in the blanks to get a better picture!

> WHEN THE _____ COMES, HE WILL GUIDE YOU INTO ALL THE _____, FOR HE WILL NOT SPEAK ON HIS OWN AUTHORITY, BUT WHATEVER HE HEARS HE WILL SPEAK, AND HE WILL DECLARE TO YOU THE THINGS THAT ARE TO COME.
> JOHN 16:13 ESV

That means that the Holy Spirit is the carrier of the voice of God to us. AND He's essential to understand and wear the belt of truth. We can't wear the belt of truth without the Holy Spirit. He's necessary to wearing the armor of God, like it can't be assembled without Him!

The Holy Spirit is the conduit that carries the voice and wisdom of God to the heart of man. He doesn't say what He wants but only what the Father speaks. Not only that, but check out the last part of that verse, "he will declare to you the things that are to come." He leads us and guides us, preparing us for what's ahead. This is so powerful.

Maybe you're asking yourself. *How do I know if it's the Holy Spirit revealing things to me and not just my own thoughts?* You know by whether or not it can be backed by the Word of God. The voice of God—the guidance of the Holy Spirit—and the written Word of God will never contradict each other. The more time you spend reading the Bible, in prayer, and being alone with God, the more you know His character and His voice.

With time you begin to learn and know the Voice of Truth, it becomes a familiar whisper that you long for and cherish oh so much.

Finish today by recalling what Jesus said:

> "MY SHEEP _____ MY _____,
> AND I KNOW THEM, AND THEY FOLLOW ME."
> JOHN 10:27 ESV

Journaling

SECRET PLACE TRAINING

Take some time this week to sit and read the truth of God, then sit and listen to what the Spirit of truth, the Holy Spirit begins to speak and stir in you. When you open your Word, ask Him to guide you into the truth. Let Him draw you closer to Jesus and allow for intimate moments of worship, conversation, and surrender.

Be sure to journal what He says so you can revisit it in the future.

Journaling

DAY THREE
knowing the truth

As we're unpacking the belt of truth, so far we've discerned multiple things. Jesus is the truth. Jesus is the Word. The Holy Spirit guides us into truth and is the Spirit of truth. He is the voice of God in our life and the One who teaches us we are God's children, and He is our Father. We know the truth is the Word of God. In order to wear the belt of truth, we need to be in the Word of God regularly. Look through these scriptures and fill in the blanks.

> SO JESUS SAID TO THE JEWS WHO HAD BELIEVED HIM, "IF YOU ABIDE IN _____, YOU ARE TRULY MY DISCIPLES, AND YOU WILL KNOW THE _____, AND THE _____ WILL SET YOU FREE."
> JOHN 8:31-32 ESV

How can we know the truth?

How do we abide in His Word?

As we spend time in the Secret Place with God reading the Bible we know the truth, we spend time with Truth (Jesus), and we learn what the truth is by reading what God says! What is the end product of knowing the truth (last part of the verses above)?

Reading the Word, spending time with Jesus and abiding in the scriptures really isn't about checking off a good Christian to-do list, it is about our freedom!! Jesus states it clear as day, the Word helps us know the truth and that truth sets us free. God has always been about us walking in freedom! How good is He? Wearing the belt of truth helps us walk freely! Turn in your Bible and see what Galatians 5:1 say about this very subject?

> IT IS FOR _____ THAT CHRIST HAS SET US FREE. STAND FIRM, THEN, AND DO NOT LET YOURSELVES BE BURDENED AGAIN BY A YOKE OF SLAVERY.
> GALATIANS 5:1 NIV

This piece of the armor of God fits together so perfectly because it is the truth that sets us free and keeps us free. Knowing the Word reminds of our identity in Christ and what He accomplished for us on the cross. He came to set us free from slavery to sin. Abide in the Word constantly and remind yourself, you are clothed in Christ! You've been forgiven, made holy, and righteous because of what Jesus did. You are no longer bound to sin but bound to righteousness. Knowing this keeps you Armored Up!

SECRET PLACE Training

Do you find it hard to decipher the truth in today's society?

Do you tend to look for truth in other places besides the Word of God?

How can you do better in making God's Word the ultimate source of truth in your life?

This week make a commitment to the Lord to spend more time in His Word—your freedom depends on it. What can you do? Read a verse a day? Read a chapter a day? Make the goal attainable and start abiding!

Journaling

Journaling

DAY FOUR
believing God's Word

All week we've been learning about the truth. The Word of God is our ultimate source and foundation of truth. We don't let society define it when God already has! For further confirmation, what does John seventeen say about this?

> "SANCTIFY THEM BY THE
> _____;
> YOUR _____ IS TRUTH."
> JOHN 17:17 NIV

Putting on the belt of truth is deciding to believe God's Word over what everyone else says and even what our eyes see. Abraham lived this way! When the Lord informed him that Sarah, his wife, would have a baby in her old (well-past-child-bearing) age, he essentially replied, "Okay." Nowadays if we heard God was going to do something impossible we're tempted to give Him all the facts of our circumstance to prove why it's not possible. What was Abraham's secret to believing the impossible? He believed the words of God over his reality. He had so much faith in the One who made the promise, that He saw the world's limitations as meaningless. Abraham had the attitude: If God said it, I believe it, end of story. And this set him apart, eventually earning Him the nickname the father of faith.

We must have this same attitude. Our facts, our situations, while they may be what we see, if it isn't what God has said we need to declare His Word and solutions over the circumstance. We must believe the One who said it is faithful. In the previous scripture it starts with the word "sanctify."

RESEARCH MORE

Sanctify is the Greek word *hagiazó*: to make holy, consecrate, sanctify, set apart [2]

Now we know we are already made holy because of what Jesus did for us, and the second we put our faith in Him we became set apart, a holy people. But this verse opens up another important element about wearing the belt of truth. As we spend time in the Word, reading the truth, it sanctifies us, both training us in the character of Christ and sets us . . .

apart/makes us different, teaching us to react differently to circumstances—doctor reports, the news. His Word is our source of truth and our supernatural reality, beyond what the eye can see. His Word teaches us to "walk by faith, not by sight." This sets us apart.

And the Word became flesh and dwelt among us, and we have seen his glory, glory as of the only Son from the Father, full of grace and truth. John 1:14 ESV

We read this quote recently, "If you don't fill your mind with the Word of God, the enemy will fill it with fear, anxiety, stress, worry, and temptation."

Our very life depends on us filling ourselves with the truth. Look up the following passages and read through them and/or write them down.

THE WORD:

REVEALS JESUS TO US
John 5:39

GUIDES US
Psalm 119:105

TEACHES, CORRECTS, CONVICTS, AND TRAINS US
2 Timothy 3:16

HELPS US OVERCOME SIN
Psalm 119:11

TEACHES US TO WORRY LESS
Isaiah 41:10

GIVES US HOPE
Psalm 119:114

HELPS US DISCERN
Hebrews 4:12

Wearing the belt of truth is many things. By spending time in the Word, being with the Word (Jesus), believing the Word, hiding the Word in our heart, asking the Holy Spirit to unpack the Word for us, and declaring the Word teaches us to live by truth. Without the belt of truth, the armor doesn't work. We have to understand and know the truth for every other piece of the armor to be effective.

SECRET PLACE *Training*

It's time to put on the belt of truth. No more letting the world or circumstance dictate our lives, we're going to let the Word of God shape our reality. What specific situations in your life do you need to declare and prophesy Bible verses over this week? Write them down on notecards, sticky notes, whatever you have, and then ask the Holy Spirit to guide you in truth, revealing the truth over these circumstances. Find a scripture for each situation you are facing, put on the belt of truth and use it!

(Ex. As for me and my house, we will serve the Lord Joshua 24:15 ESV. This is a great scripture to declare and prophesy over your home if there is strife or anyone under your roof not serving Jesus. Speak it, post it, and declare it out loud standing firm in faith that the enemy has to bow at the Word of Jesus because Jesus is the Word of God.)

Journaling

Journaling

BREASTPLATE OF RIGHTEOUSNESS
NEW COVENANT VS. OLD COVENANT

week three

Stand firm then with the belt of truth buckled around your waist with the breastplate of righteousness in place.

EPHESIANS 6:14

It was a typical day, nothing extraordinary planned for the morning. I did what I normally do on days like that—grabbed my cup of coffee and sat with my Bible and notebook. I was doing what most moms of littles do, get their alone time in before the kiddos wake.

As I sat at my dining room table praying, something different occurred. Typically, I pray with my eyes shut, and it's, well, dark. But, during this prayer, that changed. God showed me something amazing. As I began to pray, my surroundings completely transformed before me. With my eyes closed tight, the darkness suddenly turned to light, and I was in a room. It was just a room, but the most beautiful one I have ever seen. I found myself standing in the middle of this box of beauty. Now, I didn't actually go anywhere, but it's as if I was there, standing in this outrageously gorgeous space. It was so magnificent—it surpassed anything I have ever experienced with my own eyes. It was absolutely breathtaking. The joy I felt from being in this room transcended any earthly experience I've ever had. Not only was it . . . stunning, but I was overflowing with peace and wonder.

As I began to take a few steps forward, I became filled with an overwhelming excitement of what I saw; something I'd never seen in all my life. At the front of this room was the most beautiful, ornate banquet table I had ever seen. Fixer Upper ain't got nothin' on this room or this table. It was fit for a queen if you will. This table stretched across the whole front of the room. It was massive, the most enormous table imaginable. It just kept going and it was breathtaking. Stunning, gold, and shimmering. This gorgeous table was overflowing with something even more magnificent, something so precious that my mind could not even begin to comprehend. Hanging over the edges and cascading all along the front and sides of this table were gifts, but not just any gifts. These were the most beautifully wrapped packages my eyes had ever beheld.

They were stacked, staggered, and covering every square inch of space this table had to offer. The presents were too many to . . .

count, too dazzling for words to describe, and I didn't even know what was in them.

The table's lavishness drew me closer. As I made my way toward it, trying to take everything in, I noticed a detail that I'll never forget. Every one of these gifts had my name on them (spelled correctly, too). Now mind you, this was not the typical birthday or Christmas spread. This was different, special. But why? For what? What was this all about? After observing for a few moments, I moved forward to grab a gift; how could I resist? But just as I reached my arm out, BAM!!! I hit something. I tried again but was stopped a second time. I stepped back, and from floor to ceiling, side to side, I noticed a barrier wall as clear as one could imagine. I wouldn't have noticed it if I hadn't hit it time and time again, trying to take what was clearly laid out for me.

And, just as quickly as it had started, suddenly, the vision was done. It was over. I opened my eyes and immediately wrote every detail down. I was sobbing, overwhelmed with whatever it was I had just experienced. This was a first for me. I'd never been shown something so beautiful and unique.

I was confused but in a curious way. What did I just see? Over the next few weeks, God began to reveal I needed to break down the wall—but how?

Then one morning during another quiet time, I closed my eyes and began to see that room again! Everything was exactly the same as before, everything but the wall. This time the glass barricade wasn't so transparent. This time my wall was covered in words, dark heavy words. Even now, tears flood my eyes just reminiscing about it. It was dreadful. As I began to read through them, I realized very quickly exactly what it was. It was me! There it was written out, my identity, the way I saw myself, and it was sad. The words were a mix of actions of others that I had allowed to shape and mold me, past regrets, shame, hurt, rejection, and fear. I saw words that represented the choices I had made and had allowed to become my identity. These were things I kept deep down, many things no one knew but me. There it stood, this wall of ugly standing in front of me, preventing me from receiving all God had for me.

They were stacked, staggered, and covering every square inch of space this table had to offer. The presents were too many to count, too dazzling for words to describe, and I didn't even know what was in them.

I realized right then and there my identity was not in Jesus, it was in those words smeared all over that glass wall. God began teaching me how to replace those labels, lies, and agreements with what He said, and I learned to see myself clothed in Jesus, not in what the world said, or what I did.

When I saw myself like God did the wall came crashing down! It became crystal clear that I could not live on both sides of the wall—I had to choose to either live Jesus-focused or self-focused. Walking in my old identity, carrying around those heavy words, my sin and shame, hindered my destiny, but when God taught me about my "righteous in Christ" identity I began overcoming obstacle after obstacle!

Wearing the protection of Jesus, the armor of God helped me step into all God had for me and I just know it will do the same for you! So come on, let's go get our gifts, let's Armor Up, and rip open all He has for us.

— Dianne

NEW COVENANT VS. OLD COVENANT

Scan for session three video

SESSION THREE NOTES:

DAY ONE
New Covenant identity

We're nicknaming the next few sessions the "weeks of fire." If there is one topic that our hearts burn to share it's this one—that the people of God would truly understand their identity in Christ. Now, we realize this is a "buzz phrase" in Christianity, so we hope to afford some clarity. What does "identity in Christ" mean? We're so glad you asked.

The Oxford language dictionary defines it as: **identity-the fact of being who or what a person or thing is.**[3] Knowing our identity in Christ is a realization of who and what we are based on what Jesus did for us. Before we had a Savior, our identity was perhaps fully in ourselves, what we did, our family, the roles we held, the school we went to, etc . . . While these are facts about our life, this isn't who we truly are at our core. If it can be taken away or changed, it shouldn't be a part of our identity—otherwise we'd have an identity crisis every time our life or circumstances change, and some do.

Who we are in Christ never changes, and here is the great thing, it isn't based on us! Our identity in Christ is not about any role we hold or responsibility, it's not about gifts or talents, it has nothing to do with behavior or what church we attend. It's again ALL about Jesus. Shocker I know.

As we unpack the breastplate of righteousness, we pray your heart would begin to leap with joy as you grasp what it truly means to be righteous in Christ—we know ours did and still does! If we could sit around a table with a hot cup of coffee and chat about the outpouring of God's revelation on this topic, we could go on for days—there's just so much to discover.

Righteousness might sound boring, and churchy, but can we just tell you it is not. It is actually a life-altering, praise-bringing, Jesus-glorifying piece of the armor. Because sitting in person isn't possible, let's dive into the breastplate of righteousness and all the beauty it holds throughout the next few pages.

What is righteousness?

Plain and simple, righteousness is having right standing with God.

Throughout the Bible there were two ways to become righteous. One was strived for through the pages of the Old Testament and the other was brought through Jesus and we find out how in the New Testament. The latter is where we find the New Covenant believers have with God, and this is the covenant we are still living under today. (Side note . . . this is very important to understand.)

Check out the Old Covenant's way of being right with God by turning to the following scripture and filling in the blank.

> GIVE THE FOLLOWING INSTRUCTIONS TO THE PEOPLE OF _____. WHEN YOU PRESENT
> AN _____ AS AN OFFERING TO THE LORD, YOU MAY TAKE IT FROM YOUR HERD OF CATTLE OR YOUR FLOCK OF SHEEP AND GOATS. IF THE ANIMAL YOU PRESENT AS A BURNT OFFERING IS FROM THE HERD, IT MUST BE A MALE WITH NO DEFECTS. BRING IT TO THE ENTRANCE OF THE TABERNACLE SO YOU MAY BE _____ BY THE LORD. LAY YOUR HAND ON THE . . .
> ANIMAL'S HEAD, AND THE LORD WILL ACCEPT ITS DEATH IN YOUR PLACE TO PURIFY YOU, MAKING YOU
> _____.
> LEVITICUS 1:2-4 NLT

Who were these instructions given to?

How did you get right with God in the Old Testament?

It's very clear there was only system of atonement—being declared right with God—is either perfect obedience or (since that was literally impossible) by having an acceptable sacrifice to cover sin.

Can you imagine having to do this regularly? First, you would have had to live so sin-focused, so you knew when to make a sacrifice. Then, you would have had to put a lot of effort into getting . . .

the perfect sacrifice, whether you raised the animal yourself or bought it. It would have cost you a lot of time, energy, and/or money. Remember, the sacrifice had to be perfect, the best of the best. You'd then have to take the journey to the temple and wait for the priest to accept your sacrifice and then offer your sacrifice to the LORD for forgiveness and the cleansing of your sin. Once this was done, then and only then, could you have right standing with God. You would then be deemed righteous. But for how long? One week? One day? Who are we kidding? Five minutes? Basically, you'd have peace until the next sin and ooooops, have to go "get right" again.

Okay, now let's check out the New Covenant way of being right with God . . .

Look up this scripture in the New Living Translation for a very clear understanding.

> FOR NO ONE CAN EVER BE MADE _____ BY DOING WHAT THE LAW COMMANDS. THE LAW SIMPLY SHOWS US HOW _____ WE ARE. BUT NOW GOD HAS SHOWN US A WAY TO _____ WITH HIM WITHOUT KEEPING THE REQUIREMENTS OF THE LAW, AS WAS PROMISED IN THE WRITINGS OF MOSES AND THE PROPHETS LONG AGO.
> ROMANS 3:20-21 NLT

Hold the phone. The law simply shows us what?! Our sin. Remember the Old Covenant's way of being right with God required a constant awareness of sin. The law just exposes it, and the verse goes on to say there is a way to be right with God without keeping the requirements of the law (which includes the ten commandments by the way). But how could we ever be right with God without following the rules? Well, this is where the gospel comes in!

> WE ARE MADE _____ BY PLACING OUR FAITH IN _____. AND THIS IS TRUE FOR EVERYONE WHO _____, NO MATTER WHO WE ARE. FOR EVERYONE HAS SINNED; WE ALL FALL SHORT OF GOD'S GLORIOUS STANDARD. YET GOD, IN HIS _____, FREELY _____ IN HIS SIGHT. HE DID THIS THROUGH _____ WHEN HE FREED US FROM THE PENALTY FOR OUR SINS.
> ROMANS 3:22-24 NLT

WHAT did that just say? We are made right with God/righteous by placing our faith in who, in what? Our behavior? How we dress? What denomination we are a part of? NO! By placing our faith in Jesus. Our righteousness and how we become right with God is by faith in Christ alone, not any other way!!! This is the grace of God—

He gifted us something we could never earn. *This just makes me want to stop and have a praise break!*

We're right with God through Jesus Christ—He accomplished it through Him only, and He doesn't need us to add to it. **Jesus is a BIG deal.** The biggest, actually. This is literally the best news ever. Jesus did all the work, He bore all our shame, and all our sin. He took on everything that would ever keep us from being righteous before God and He took it to the cross. He is our ransom. He's is our freedom. He is our way, he is the only way. Because of what Jesus did we are free! *Amen!!*

What are some tangible things that you can do to help keep yourself Jesus-focused?

(Remember we need to take our eyes off us and keep them on our sacrifice. In the Leviticus passage you'll notice that the priest wasn't looking at the person to be atoned for his sin, he was examining the sacrifice the person brought.

God is looking to see if we are covered in the sacrifice of his Son. That's the only thing that makes us righteous.)

We stepped into the New Covenant the second we put our faith in Jesus Christ. When we are living from a New Covenant mindset, we realize it is our belief in Him—His death as our sacrifice, in our place—no matter our sin, makes us right with God. Our righteousness will never again be based on anything we do, but completely hinges on what Jesus did for us. BELIEVE THAT! If you are still living under a "works" theology or an Old Covenant mindset thinking you need to "do" something to get right with God again, today we want to show you the freedom that is available in Christ. We're right with God because of Jesus, trust in your Savior's covering. Thank Him for His redemptive work on the cross! This is how we adequately wear the breastplate of righteousness—understanding we're righteous by faith!

SECRET PLACE TRAINING

Grab a black pen and a red pen or marker. Make a list of all of your shortcomings and struggles/things you just can't seem to get victory over. Now lay them at the feet of Jesus. Pull out a red pen/marker and write over that list: Covered by the blood of Jesus! There is no sin or obstacle that Jesus hasn't paid for! He covered every shortcoming and removed it from your account! Through Him we have overcome.

Now, have an honest conversation with the Lord, *Father, when I look at myself I see all my shortcomings, but when you look at me, what do you see? Help me change my perspective. Help me stop being sin-focused and start being Jesus-focused. Give me a revelation of the work of my Savior.*

Remember, when we focus on being a sinner the fruit is sin, but when we focus on being surrendered to Jesus it's the fruit of the Spirit that we get.

Journaling

DAY TWO
New Covenant vs. Old Covenant

We have been completely freed from a behavior-based relationship with God. Hallelujah! Because of Jesus, we have the beautiful gift of living under the New Covenant. The enemy would love to keep you in a works-mindset (this includes having thoughts like: *God will bless me if I do _____, I am righteous if I have obeyed enough*). The constant belief that you have to be good enough to be accepted by God, that you have to be perfect to be right with Him is really self-righteousness—a right standing with God that you have achieved yourself. First of all, that's exhausting and secondly, it's absolutely unattainable and the enemy knows this. We don't want to live in self-righteousness; we want to live from His righteousness. Yesterday, we began unpacking the different ways to get right with God in the Old Covenant and the New Covenant—keep in mind it is impossible to live under both covenants at the same time. We are either living under the law or under freedom. Under the old or under the new, self-focused or Jesus-focused.

Thoughts

Old Way vs New Way

Let's recap differences between the Old Covenant and the New Covenant.

As you look through the list, get honest with yourself and the Lord, ask: *Which of these attributes describe me?* Circle the words you resonate with. This list is very telling about what covenant mindset we have. Often we find we're living from both, but we intend to renew our minds with the truth of the New Covenant!

OLD COVENANT	NEW COVENANT
Self-focused	Jesus-focused
works based	based on the work of Jesus
pride	humility
self-righteousness	God's righteousness
never enough	more than enough in Christ
heavy	His yolk is light
burdensome	blessing
identity in my works	identity in Christ
slavery/fear	freedom
death	life
condemnation	approval
judgemental	gracious, kind, peaceful
rude	loving
angry	joyful
unbelief, curse	faith, hope
slave	child
timid	bold
anxious	sound mind
religious	relationship
division	unity
self-effort	Holy Spirit help

Our heart is to highlight the righteousness of God on display in the New Covenant, it is the way to be right with God by faith, not work, not behavior, not obedience. This New Covenant way is different than the Old Covenant way, and Paul unpacks it clearly in second Corinthians three. Just go ahead and read the whole chapter. Pay attention to what He says about the old way, which is the Old Covenant, and how different it is from the new way. Meet us back here and we'll do some fill in the blanks to bring the truth home.

> HE HAS ENABLED US TO BE MINISTERS OF HIS _____. THIS IS A COVENANT NOT OF WRITTEN LAWS, BUT OF THE _____. THE OLD WRITTEN COVENANT ENDS IN _____; BUT UNDER THE NEW COVENANT, THE SPIRIT GIVES _____.
> 2 CORINTHIANS 3:6 NLT

Just a couple things here. We are ministers of what?

It's not a covenant of written laws, rules, and regulations is it? It's a covenant of what?

Have you ever heard the New Covenant as a covenant of the Spirit? How interesting is that?

Okay two more things, the Old Covenant ends in what?

Now under the New Covenant, the Spirit of God gives what?

See how important it is to have a New Covenant understanding and mindset? It seems to be a matter of life and death.

> NOW IF THE MINISTRY OF _____, CARVED IN LETTERS ON STONE, CAME WITH SUCH GLORY THAT THE ISRAELITES COULD NOT GAZE AT MOSES' FACE BECAUSE OF ITS GLORY, WHICH WAS BEING BROUGHT TO AN END, WILL NOT THE MINISTRY OF THE _____ HAVE EVEN MORE GLORY? FOR IF THERE WAS GLORY IN THE MINISTRY OF _____, THE MINISTRY OF _____ MUST FAR EXCEED IT IN GLORY.
> 2 CORINTHIANS 3:7-9 ESV

Okay, Paul was not holding his punches here. He spoke of the Old Covenant twice with two very telling words.

What did He call the Old Covenant?

The ministry of _____ and the ministry of _____.

Wow. That is pretty intense, okay in contrast what did he refer to the New Covenant as?

The ministry of _____ and the ministry of _____.

Isn't it interesting that one huge difference between the Old and New Covenants is that the latter comes with a gift from God to walk in His ways: The Holy Spirit. The New Covenant is the ministry of the Spirit and the ministry of righteousness! This is what we've been called to do: Walk in the power of the Spirit and we have the ministry of telling people anyone can be made right with God because of what Jesus did. This is some good news!!

It's becoming crystal clear that to truly wear the breastplate of righteousness is in fact having the New Covenant mindset: Understanding we're right with God because of Jesus—righteous by faith in Him—and we can walk in God's ways because of His Spirit living in us.

SECRET PLACE Training

Spend some time processing all of this with the Lord. Whichever side of the covenants you've identified more with, ask the Father to help you stand fully in this position of being a minister of the New Covenant. Ask Him to tear down any veils you may have up that have kept you from understanding the good news or prevented you from sharing it. Do you feel unqualified to be called a minister, perhaps thinking this only applies to pastors? Ask the Lord to reaffirm the truth that ALL of His kids have been commissioned as ministers of the gospel and called to fulfill the great commision. Write down what you feel the Lord reveals.

Journaling

DAY THREE
self-righteousness or His righteousness

Our perspective matters. This week is so foundational in understanding how to accurately wear the breastplate of righteousness. In order for us to rest secure in this piece of the armor we're highlighting the difference in the way of being righteous under the Old Covenant vs. the New Covenant. The Apostle Paul contrasted it a few times, let's see how he described it in Galatians chapter four.

Read through the following verses and fill in the blanks, keep in mind when the Bible uses the phrase "under the law" it means living in an Old Covenant mindset, believing in Jesus but simultaneously believing behavior maintains your righteousness.

> TELL ME, YOU WHO WANT TO LIVE UNDER THE _____, DO YOU KNOW WHAT THE LAW ACTUALLY SAYS? THE SCRIPTURES SAY THAT ABRAHAM HAD TWO SONS, ONE FROM HIS _____ WIFE AND ONE FROM HIS _____ WIFE. THE SON OF THE SLAVE WIFE WAS BORN IN A _____ TO BRING ABOUT THE FULFILLMENT OF GOD'S PROMISE. BUT THE SON OF THE FREEBORN WIFE WAS BORN AS _____ OF HIS PROMISE.
> GALATIANS 4:21-23 NLT

Okay let's just pause for a quick minute. Most believers are familiar with the whole Abraham, Sarah, and Hagar debacle . . . but on the chance someone reading isn't, let's summarize and get on the same page. God promised Abraham, who was about seventy five years old at the time, that his wife, Sarah, was going to have a son. She was barren and WAY past birthing years, and probably already had menopause . . . so medically impossible. But God. God specializes in the impossible, but after a few years the baby had not come, so Abraham and Sarah decided to solve the problem through "their own effort." Abraham had a child with Sarah's servant who was not free. The child of their union was named Ishmael and he was not the true heir of Abraham or the promise of God. Many years after Ishmael was born Sarah finally got pregnant miraculously—the problem of Sarah's barrenness was solved through "God's effort." With Isaac, God made it happen, God did it! With Ishmael, humans made it happen, they did it. (See Genesis 15-21 for the whole story.) Okay, what does this have to do with the Old and New Covenants? Check out the next scriptures:

> THESE TWO WOMEN SERVE AS AN ILLUSTRATION OF GOD'S TWO _____ THE FIRST WOMAN, HAGAR, REPRESENTS MOUNT SINAI WHERE PEOPLE RECEIVED THE LAW THAT _____ THEM. AND NOW JERUSALEM IS JUST LIKE MOUNT SINAI IN ARABIA, BECAUSE SHE AND HER CHILDREN LIVE IN _____ TO THE LAW. BUT THE OTHER WOMAN, SARAH, REPRESENTS THE HEAVENLY JERUSALEM. SHE IS THE _____ WOMAN, AND SHE IS OUR MOTHER.
> GALATIANS 4:24-26 NLT

What do the women represent?

Hagaar represents:

Sarah represents:

The Old Covenant kept the people in:

The New Covenant set the people:

Let's recap what this passage is saying and how it connects to righteousness. This week, we've been pointing out that there are two ways to be right with God. Human effort and earned, or Jesus' effort and received as a gift. The first is the Old Covenant way of righteousness, the second is the New Covenant way. Did you see how Ishmael and his mother Hagar represent the Old Covenant? He was conceived through "man's effort,"(self-righteousness) while Isaac and his mother represent the New Covenant. Isaac was born of "God's effort" (His righteousness) a foreshadow of Jesus' work on the cross and His resurrection. God achieved righteousness for us!

When we live under the law, we have a slave mentality, but when we live under grace we have a son mentality. In ancient times, slaves were much different than sons. Slaves could not inherit, only sons could, slaves did not have authority of their master, but sons had the authority of their father. The Old Covenant is a slave mentality while the New Covenant is a son mentality. To truly wear the breastplate of righteousness, inherit the promises, and walk in authority we must understand we aren't slaves but sons (or daughters depending on who is reading this)!

SECRET PLACE Training

Look up Romans 8:15 and write it in the space provided. What spirit did we receive according to this scripture?

Since how we view ourselves matters, consider what mindset you have been living under? Do you find yourself being "me" focused and constantly trying to be perfect and acceptable based on what you do? If so, write out why you think this way and then lay them at the feet of Jesus and surrender that mindset to him.

Then, ask Him to reveal to you the truth of what it means to live in the freedom of sonship that comes from Him alone. (FYI-Paul used the word son to describe all the children of God, because sons were the only ones who received an inheritance in those days—it's conferring inheritance not gender, it applies to women too! Women deal with being called 'sons', while the guys have to deal with being called the 'bride' of Christ. Haha! Both terms apply to both genders.)

Journaling

DAY FOUR
righteousness is a gift

Gifts aren't earned. All week we've been talking about the differences of righteousness between the Old & New Covenants. In the Old Testament, being right with God was not a gift, it was absolutely earned. Even the verbiage of the ten commandments displays the importance of human effort. Let's look at a few, and fill in the blanks:

> _____SHALL HAVE NO OTHER GODS BEFORE ME . . .
> _____SHALL NOT MAKE FOR YOURSELF A CARVED IMAGE . . .
> _____SHALL NOT TAKE THE NAME OF THE LORD YOUR GOD IN VAIN . . .
> _____SHALL NOT COMMIT ADULTERY . . .
> _____SHALL NOT BEAR FALSE WITNESS AGAINST YOUR NEIGHBOR . . .
> EXODUS 20:3, 4, 7, 14, 16 ESV

Whose effort is highlighted here?

Okay, now look at this passage in Jeremiah revealing the terms of Old Covenant:

> REMIND THE PEOPLE OF JUDAH AND JERUSALEM ABOUT THE TERMS OF MY _____ WITH THEM. SAY TO THEM, 'THIS IS WHAT THE LORD, THE GOD OF ISRAEL, SAYS: _____ IS ANYONE WHO DOES NOT _____THE TERMS OF MY COVENANT! FOR I SAID TO YOUR ANCESTORS WHEN I BROUGHT THEM OUT OF THE IRON-SMELTING FURNACE OF EGYPT, "IF _____ ME AND _____WHATEVER I COMMAND YOU, _____ YOU WILL BE MY PEOPLE, AND I WILL BE YOUR GOD."
> JEREMIAH 11:2-4 NLT

Again, we see whose obedience the covenant focuses on. Was the blessing and curses up to God or you?

Personally, we are really glad we don't live under this system . . . it makes us REAL grateful for Jesus! Although, if we're not careful, we might be talked into believing we still relate to God this way. Religions all over the world operate in this system promising: *If "you" follow these rules then you'll be accepted by God and go to Heaven.* But this is Old Covenant teaching. Any way to the Father except through what Jesus did is works-based, it is not grace. We may have grown up believing our relationship with God was up to our behavior, but sometimes we have to unlearn some mindsets and teachings to truly experience the freedom Christ has to offer. Let's now turn to the New Covenant and read it for ourselves.

Fill in the blanks and pay attention to who the covenant focuses on.

> HE [JESUS] _____
> THE FIRST COVENANT IN ORDER TO PUT THE SECOND INTO EFFECT. FOR GOD'S WILL WAS FOR US TO BE MADE _____ BY THE SACRIFICE OF THE BODY OF _____, ONCE FOR ALL TIME. UNDER THE _____, THE PRIEST STANDS AND MINISTERS BEFORE THE ALTAR DAY AFTER DAY OFFERING THE SAME SACRIFICES AGAIN AND AGAIN, WHICH . . .

> CAN _____ TAKE AWAY SINS. BUT OUR HIGH PRIEST OFFERED HIMSELF TO GOD AS A SINGLE SACRIFICE FOR SINS, GOOD FOR _____. THEN HE SAT DOWN IN THE PLACE OF HONOR AT GOD'S RIGHT HAND. THERE HE WAITS UNTIL HIS ENEMIES ARE HUMBLED AND MADE A FOOTSTOOL UNDER HIS FEET.
> FOR BY THAT ONE OFFERING _____ FOREVER MADE _____ THOSE WHO ARE BEING MADE HOLY.
> AND THE HOLY SPIRIT ALSO TESTIFIES THAT THIS IS SO. FOR HE SAYS,
> "THIS IS THE NEW COVENANT ____ WILL MAKE WITH MY PEOPLE ON THAT DAY, SAYS THE LORD:
> ____ WILL PUT MY LAWS IN THEIR HEARTS, AND
> ____ WILL WRITE THEM ON THEIR MINDS." THEN HE SAYS,
> ____ WILL NEVER AGAIN REMEMBER THEIR SINS AND LAWLESS DEEDS."
> AND WHEN _____, THERE IS NO NEED TO OFFER ANY MORE SACRIFICES.
> HEBREWS 10:9B-18 NLT

Who is doing all the work in the New Covenant?

73

This is a covenant based on Jesus, y'all! Not us. It is crystal clear. We are just benefitting from what Jesus did for us. Notice the difference in the verbiage between the covenants? You shall vs. I will. God was like, "Nah, this is not working, I will be fixing the problem, and it won't have a thing to do with y'all because you just can't. You, for real, need a Savior!" And we did. And we have one. Do you see how Jesus' one sacrifice perfects us forever, and forgives our sins forever?! His blood covers and removes our sins for eternity, even the ones we haven't even committed yet! Our forgiveness and holiness and righteousness are all based on His work, not ours! This is the best news ever! The Old Covenant was a relationship with God they had to *earn*. The New Covenant is a relationship with God that we are *gifted* because of Jesus.

And here is where we are trying to get to: we always live FROM our identity. So, if we think we're dirty, rotten sinners, even after we've been made anew in Christ . . . first: we aren't acknowledging the work of Jesus. He remembers our sins no more and He does not see us that way! He's actually made us a new creation, a righteous, holy, perfected creation, based on His work. Secondly, if we view ourselves incorrectly, we will live incorrectly.

We will live up to our identity, so we will keep staying stuck in sin cycles if we see ourselves as sinners—ignoring the cross and resurrection. BUT if we see ourselves through the lens of the New Covenant, righteous because of Jesus, Holy because of Jesus, perfected because of Jesus . . . guess how we start living? Righteous. Holy. Perfected. Do we still mess up? Yes. But our mess-ups no longer define us, Jesus does! His blood speaks a better word about us!

We can stand against all the schemes of the enemy when we have the breastplate of our righteous identity guarding our hearts. As a matter of fact, we'll end with a very famous scripture that is based on knowing this truth, look it up and fill in the blanks:

> "NO _____ FORMED AGAINST YOU SHALL _____, AND EVERY TONGUE WHICH RISES AGAINST YOU IN JUDGMENT YOU SHALL CONDEMN. THIS IS THE HERITAGE OF THE SERVANTS OF THE LORD, AND THEIR _____ IS FROM ME," SAYS THE LORD.
> ISAIAH 54:17 NKJV

It is important to notice the weapon will be formed, but it will not prosper in our lives when we have an awareness of where our righteousness comes from. Where is that (according to the previous scripture)?

The only reason we're righteous is because this is a gift God gave us. A lot of times the weapon prospers in our life because we think our right standing with God is up to us, and we live in shame & condemnation—which leads to a lot of other problems—or we try to get God to answer our prayer because we've been "good enough." Now we haven't. But Jesus has, and there is no other name by which we can ask. We dismantle attacks when we know our righteousness is from God! Get the breastplate of righteousness in place friends and stop the enemy's weapons from working!

SECRET PLACE Training

Spend some time with the Lord processing the difference between the covenants and ask Him what He is trying to teach you. Have you thought "being right with God" is something you had to constantly earn, or did you know it was a gift all along? Look up Romans 5:17 and write down what righteousness is listed as? Earned or gifted? Next, read what happens when a person receives it as a gift. Do they live defeated or in victory? Lastly, ask the Lord if you have truly received it as a gift, or if you still need to. Ask Him to teach you more about this!

Journaling

Journaling

BREASTPLATE OF RIGHTEOUSNESS
CORNERSTONE
week four

Stand firm then with the belt of truth buckled around your waist with the breastplate of righteousness in place.

EPHESIANS 6:14

Lord, I am so frustrated, I do not understand this. What does this even mean? As I sat there continuing to read the same verse over and over I knew there was something deeper, something I wasn't grasping. I didn't necessarily know how to get that understanding but I was determined to find out. I had my coffee ready, my worship music going, Bible open, and I was going in. Join me in my conversation with God as I discovered His righteousness while sitting at my dining room table.

"I am the righteousness of God through Christ Jesus." I said outloud again and again. I must have repeated this phrase ten times before frustration set in, I mean, I sounded like a broken record. Let me clarify, I wasn't frustrated with God, I was however, completely irritated with myself. Why? Because I realized that I didn't truly understand these power packed words of wisdom that were supposed to make all the difference in the world for me. So yes, I was frustrated that I could not understand this particular truth of God in my flesh. As much as I tried, my understanding lacked His supernatural wisdom. So I just blurted out "God, what does this mean? What does it mean that I am the righteousness of You through Your Son? I don't get it!" Y'all, that's when it happened. Immediate breakthrough. In an instant I heard these words whispered in my Spirit "Dianne, I took your hell for you." I sobbed. Seven words, seven life changing miracle working words and my life has been forever changed. It was in that moment that my eyes were opened, and I understood that Jesus took everything that I deserved and now when the Father sees me, He sees me covered in the perfection of Jesus, not my sin. Instantly, For the first time in my life I understood what it meant to be the righteousness of God through Jesus. I finally saw myself as the Father saw me, covered in the perfection of His Son. When my Spirit heard those words, chains broke, freedom was found, and I've never looked back. Friends, He endured everything that was ours to receive. Whether we accept the gift of Jesus and His righteousness or not, He willingly gave his life for us so that we can experience the greatness of God in both the here and now and for all of eternity.

That's the promise that I'm standing on. That's the solid rock of my foundation. It's Jesus. Amen! After I grasped this truth, I realized that I had not given Jesus' credit where credit was due. I need to be jumping up and down shouting from the rooftops about this miraculous, scandalous gift of His redemptive love. He loves us just as we are but way too much to leave us that way.

— *Dianne*

CORNERSTONE

Scan for session four video

SESSION FOUR NOTES:

DAY ONE
confidence in Christ

If there is anything that needs to be shouted from the rooftops, it's this revelation right here. Come on somebody, the revelation of righteousness will change your life. We know we covered a lot about this topic last week, but the truth is, we're just getting started. Let's just say that this particular piece of the Armor of God is very layered, there's a lot to it.

Last week, we learned about the Old and New Covenants and their relationship to righteousness. It's then that we uncovered the truth that the New Covenant is actually freedom in Jesus. As we move forward, we are going to unwrap what the temple of God looks like in the New Covenant and why the foundation of that temple holds such significance. Keep in mind anytime you build anything, the foundation holds in it, the success or failure of the build. Knowing that, let's begin our study in first Peter.

> AS YOU COME TO HIM, A
> _____ _____ REJECTED
> BY MEN BUT IN THE SIGHT OF GOD
> CHOSEN AND PRECIOUS, YOU
> YOURSELVES LIKE LIVING STONES
> ARE BEING . . .

> _____ _____ AS A
> SPIRITUAL HOUSE, TO BE A HOLY
> PRIESTHOOD, TO OFFER SPIRITUAL
> SACRIFICES ACCEPTABLE TO GOD
> THROUGH JESUS CHRIST. FOR IT
> STANDS IN SCRIPTURE: "BEHOLD, I
> AM LAYING IN ZION A STONE, A
> _____ CHOSEN AND
> PRECIOUS, AND WHOEVER
> BELIEVES IN HIM WILL NOT BE PUT
> TO SHAME."
> 1 PETER 2:4-6 ESV

Let's dive in a bit. Who is the first living stone that Peter is referring to?

Who is Peter referring to the second time he mentions living stones?

What are we being built up as?

1. Spiritual _____

2. Holy _____

Who is the Cornerstone?

Friends, are you getting this? Jesus is the foundation of it all! He is our cornerstone. He is the firm foundation in which we stand. Let's keep going, fill in the missing words on this scripture found in Ephesians chapter two.

> BUILT ON THE FOUNDATION OF THE APOSTLES AND PROPHETS. _____ _____ HIMSELF BEING THE _____, IN WHOM THE WHOLE STRUCTURE, BEING JOINED TOGETHER, GROWS INTO A HOLY TEMPLE IN THE LORD. IN HIM YOU ALSO ARE BEING BUILT TOGETHER INTO A _____ PLACE FOR GOD BY THE SPIRIT.
> EPHESIANS 2:20-22 ESV

Isn't this amazing? We are the living stones, the new covenant temple of God Almighty. We are His dwelling place and again, Jesus is the Cornerstone.

> FOR NO ONE CAN LAY A _____ OTHER THAN THAT WHICH IS LAID, WHICH IS JESUS CHRIST.
> 1 CORINTHIANS 3:11 ESV

He (Jesus) said to them, But who do you say that I am? Simon Peter replied, "You are the Christ, the Son of the living God." And Jersus answered him, "Blessed are you Simon Bar-Jonah! For flesh and blood has not revealed this to you, but my Father who is in heaven. And I tell you, you are Peter, and on this rock I will build my church, and the gates of hell shall not prevail against it." Mathew 16:15-18 ESV

What is the rock that Jesus is referring to?

What can the gates of hell not prevail against?

Could it be that the "this rock" in this scripture is referring to the answer that Peter gave Jesus when he asked Peter who he was? Could it be that Jesus is telling his disciples "I am the rock that the living temple of God, I am the rock that hell can not prevail against, I am the rock, the Christ, the Son of the Living God, I am your cornerstone?"

Have you ever thought of this scripture this way?

Do you think it's possible that Jesus is referring to Himself as the rock or do you think it's Peter that Jesus is referring to building His church on.

Ask the Holy Spirit to pour out His wisdom and understanding. Ask for a fresh revelation on the building structure of the New Covenant temple of God.

SECRET PLACE TRAINING

Have you ever considered yourself the actual temple of God? It's a fascinating thought, isn't it? As you spend time with the Lord today, ask Him if there are any areas of your temple that He'd like to clean up or repair. Invite the Holy Spirit to have His way in your life. As He reveals things that no longer serve you or Him, confidently surrender each one at the feet of Jesus, knowing that you can trust Him every step of the way.

And I am certain that God, who began a good work within you, will continue his work until it is finally finished on the day when Christ Jesus returns. Philippians 1:6 NLT

Journaling

Journaling

DAY TWO
Christ the Cornerstone

What in the world is a cornerstone and why is it important? Let's talk about construction here. In building terms, the cornerstone is the rock on which the whole structure is built from. The total weight of the building rests on this particular stone, which, if removed, would cause the whole structure to collapse. Without the cornerstone, the building will not be properly aligned ultimately causing the structure to be unstable, unreliable, and unsafe.

Yesterday, we talked about how Jesus is the cornerstone in the building of God's new temple. Let's continue and see what else scripture has to say about Jesus being our cornerstone. Y'all, I don't know if this gets you excited but do you realize the confidence, we can walk in knowing that Jesus is our foundation. Come on, somebody better shout AMEN!

> WHAT SHALL WE SAY, THEN? THAT GENTILES WHO DID NOT PURSUE _____ HAVE ATTAINED IT, THAT IS, A RIGHTEOUSNESS THAT IS _____ _____; BUT THAT . . .

> ISRAEL WHO PURSUED A LAW THAT WOULD LEAD TO RIGHTEOUSNESS DID NOT SUCCEED IN REACHING THAT LAW.

Why?

> BECAUSE THEY DID NOT PURSUE IT BY FAITH, BUT AS IF IT WERE BASED _____ _____. THEY HAVE STUMBLED OVER THE STUMBLING STONE, AS IT IS WRITTEN, "BEHOLD, I AM LAYING IN ZION A STONE OF STUMBLING, AND A ROCK OF OFFENSE; AND WHOEVER _____ IN HIM WILL NOT BE PUT TO SHAME."
> ROMANS 9:30-33 ESV

What did the Gentiles attain?

Did they earn it?

Why did the Isrealites fail at attaining right standing with God?

We can clearly see that this scripture is referring to Jesus as a stone, but why does it refer to Jesus here as a stumbling stone and a rock of offense? The Word says that because they could no longer earn right standing with God based on their works, it tripped them up, they stumbled over the stone that they were called to build on. Imagine living your whole life trying to earn acceptance based on good behavior and now all of a sudden, it is no longer earned but gifted? Wouldn't that trip you up and challenge your way of life? Do you see how important it is to understand that our faith has to be rooted in the righteousness of Christ, and not in our own works? If we don't accept the gift, instead of standing on the cornerstone of His work, we'll trip over this stone and keep trying to earn it with own works.

How can you be confident that you're building on the right foundation?

What other "cornerstones" compete for your trust besides Jesus?

Just like a building rests on its cornerstone, we too can confidently rest in Jesus. We can trust that He will be our stability, our strength, and our guide. You see, Jesus united Jews and Gentiles into . . . one people when He willingly surrendered himself to die for our sins. It's because of His sacrifice that He was able to break down the wall of hostility that once separated Jews from Gentiles. Now that there is no separation, and everyone has the ability to live in Christ, those who had originally been "the chosen" ones of God, became a little offended. Now we might think this a Jew and Gentile problem, but the way the enemy sneaks this mindset into the body of Christ today is through competition. We can view other churches with an "US vs. THEM" mentality. We must know, there are not a bunch of different churches in the world, there is one church meeting at different locations. Just because we have different worship styles, denominations, and opinions doesn't mean we aren't all God's children. We are called to be one body, one bride, one church, with one LORD. Offense can creep in when we feel that only our church or group of churches is the "chosen" while others are not. But the reality is, Jesus broke down the wall of hostility between all of God's children.

The religious of Jesus' day didn't like having their rules and doctrines challenged, even though it was being challenged by God Himself. They didn't want anyone else added to their "chosen" family, so they saw Gentiles being accepted without following the law as a . . .

threat to all they'd known. They were offended! This is why Jesus was called the Rock of Offense (1 Peter 2:8).

> "BEHOLD, I AM LAYING IN ZION A STONE, A CORNERSTONE CHOSEN AND PRECIOUS, AND WHOEVER _____ WILL NOT BE PUT TO SHAME." SO THE HONOR IS FOR YOU WHO BELIEVE, BUT FOR THOSE WHO DO NOT BELIEVE, "THE STONE THAT THE BUILDERS REJECTED HAS BECOME THE CORNERSTONE," AND "A STONE OF STUMBLING, AND A ROCK OF _____." THEY STUMBLE BECAUSE THEY DISOBEY THE WORD, AS THEY WERE DESTINED TO DO.
> 1 PETER 2:6-8 ESV

Who is not put to shame?

Let's look up the word: disobey, because we need to find out what they were disobeying.

It is the Greek word: *apeitheó*: to disobey, refuse conformity, to disbelieve (wilfully and perversely) not believe, disobedient, unbelieving.[4]

RESEARCH MORE

The verse says "They stumble because they disobey the word"... this means there is a specific word or message they are "disbelieving"—which was Jesus is the Messiah who anyone could believe in to become a part of God's family, this is why they trip. It's sad but much like today, many of God's chosen got sidetracked by religion instead of living in freedom. The Messiah they had been studying, reading about, and waiting for had actually arrived—but they missed Him. The Pharisees and religious were so rigid and judgmental that it blinded them from seeing the work God was doing right in front of them.

Can you see how it's easy to get stuck in religion—stuck on the rules and regulations, stuck on denominational bylaws—and miss the very miracle of the One whom the whole Bible is about?

What does it look like for one to be stuck in the rut of religion in today's day?

How does religion affect our relationship with Jesus?

What part does religion play in disunity in the body of Christ?

Now, hopefully it's getting clear why we started the day talking about building projects and cornerstones? Y'all, God is building His temple in us, what a privilege, and we don't even have to hold the weight of it all, we simply get to put our hope and trust in the One who can, Jesus. We're all part of the same family, fighting the same battle, united by and standing firm on our King Jesus. AMEN?!

Journaling

SECRET PLACE Training

Are there certain things about Jesus or the Body of Christ that cause you to trip or stumble over Him? If so, what might they be?

If you answered yes to the above question, ask the Holy Spirit to guide you in truth and to help set your feet firmly on the Rock and to keep you from tripping.

It's okay to be honest and open when talking to the Lord. He knows your heart and wants you to know that you can trust Him with it. Be authentic, ask Him the tough questions that you wrestle with. He's not afraid of them. As a matter of fact, He welcomes them.

Journaling

Journaling

DAY THREE
revelation of righteousness

I'm not sure if you're the type that's a sucker for a good treasure hunt movie, but I am. The word of God is like following the greatest treasure map of all time. There are twists and turns, unexpected moments, cliff-hanging story lines, and treasure, lots and lots of treasure. It's a never ending journey of gaining wisdom, understanding, truth and love, all while becoming more and more like Jesus every step of the way. It's so good y'all!

If you've ever watched a treasure hunt movie then you get the concept of getting a revelation. It's as if with each clue on the map you find the hunter gaining more and more insight and understanding as the search continues. A revelation of God's word is basically the same thing. It's the revealing of something. It's making something known and the more we dive in to the Word of God the more the Holy Spirit reveals.

If you remember this week's story, Dianne was raised in the church and surrounded by Jesus loving people her whole life, yet she still personally lacked a true revelation on righteousness.

The reality is, we haven't all had a revelation, and that's okay, but just like we would be crazy to stop seeking for a treasure we had the map to, let's not stop seeking for fresh revelations in God's Word. Fill in the blank in the following scripture:

> I REJOICE IN YOUR WORD LIKE ONE WHO DISCOVERS A GREAT _____.
> PSALM 119:162 NLT

In life, what are you struggling with? This life-changing scripture holds power over every single thing you walk through!

What a blessing to know that when the Father looks at us, He sees the perfectness of His Son. We are clothed in the righteousness of Jesus, my friends. It doesn't matter what we've done or what's been done to us. God sees us perfectly covered in the righteousness of Christ—our cornerstone keeps us in right standing.

> THERE IS THEREFORE NOW _____ _____ FOR THOSE WHO ARE IN CHRIST JESUS.
> ROMANS 8:1 ESV

As long as we're aware that we're "in Christ", condemnation does not work! Come on y'all, that's something to be excited about! We can experience condemning feelings when we forget we're hidden in our Savior, covered by His blood!

Let's keep going and check out a few more scriptures on how the Bible declares that it is indeed Jesus who is our righteousness, that He is the One who makes us right with God.

> "FOR THE TIME IS COMING," SAYS THE LORD, "WHEN I WILL RAISE UP A RIGHTEOUS DESCENDANT FROM KING DAVID'S LINE. HE WILL BE A KING WHO RULES WITH WISDOM. HE WILL DO WHAT IS JUST AND RIGHT THROUGHOUT THE LAND. AND THIS WILL BE HIS NAME: 'THE _____ IS OUR _____.' IN THAT DAY JUDAH WILL BE SAVED, AND ISRAEL WILL LIVE IN SAFETY.
> JEREMIAH 23:5-6 NLT

Did you catch that? Who is our righteousness?

And who is the LORD?

We know this is referring to Jesus because He is the King of kings who did indeed come from the lineage of King David. He's the one that lived a perfect, sinless life, fully man, yet fully God. He alone had the power and the authority to take what only we deserved (punishment for sin), and give us what only He deserved (right standing with God). All because of His immense love for us. Amen to that!!!!

The LORD Jesus is our righteousness. It doesn't say He makes us act righteous, it says He IS our righteousness, meaning: He is the reason we are right with God. But an awareness of this truth leads to us acting righteous! We walk in alignment with our identity, remember?!

Let's wrap up our study today by looking up Ephesians 2:13 and be reminded once again of what it is that Jesus did.

Jesus' blood is the reason we're close to God! Our foundation is built on His sacrifice! What a firm cornerstone for us to stand on! Amen!

SECRET PLACE *Training*

Spend some time today in worship. Minimize disruptions, light a candle, put on soft worship music if you can, and fix all your attention on Jesus.

Listen to the words and message of the songs "Cornerstone," by Hillsong worship and "Firm Foundation," by Cody Carnes. Just spend some time in the presence of God worshiping the Lord thanking Him for being your firm foundation, your cornerstone.

Journaling

Journaling

DAY FOUR
firm foundation

Tornados suck y'all! It was just a few days ago that one touched down close to where we were writing this study. This storm was no joke y'all. The winds and the rains were pounding all around us, branches were falling, debris was blowing, and hail the size of golf balls were pouring down from the sky.

Storms have the ability to take out whatever is in their way. With that being said there's a particular parable that Jesus tells in the book of Mathew. Let's take a look and see what He has to say. Fill in the blanks below as you read through.

> "EVERYONE THEN WHO HEARS THESE WORDS OF MINE AND DOES THEM WILL BE LIKE A WISE MAN WHO BUILT HIS HOUSE ON THE _____. AND THE RAIN FELL, AND THE FLOODS CAME, AND THE WINDS BLEW AND BEAT ON THAT HOUSE, BUT IT DID NOT FALL, BECAUSE IT HAD BEEN FOUNDED ON THE ROCK. AND EVERYONE WHO _____ THESE _____ ____ _____ AND DOES . . .

> NOT _____ _____ WILL BE LIKE A FOOLISH MAN WHO BUILT HIS HOUSE ON THE _____. AND THE RAIN FELL, AND THE FLOODS CAME, AND THE WINDS BLEW AND BEAT AGAINST THAT HOUSE, AND IT FELL, AND GREAT WAS THE FALL OF IT."
> MATHEW 7:24-27 ESV

What does the wise man build on?

Who did we establish the "Rock" is?

I love that Jesus is straight up telling us that the wise not only build their house on Him, but they also do what He says. Let's clarify, this isn't referring to a "I have to earn my way" mentality. It's referring to righteousness and us building our lives on the bedrock of Christ.

Armor Up

Understanding that we are righteous because of the work of Christ positions us firm on the foundation of Jesus Himself. When the rain falls and the winds come and beat on our house, we will stand firm, because we have established the foundation for our spiritual home.

The foolish embrace a surface level righteousness, a sand based righteousness rooted in self and religion. It's an unstable foundation that the storms of life are certain to take out.

What storms of life have you been facing?

Do you feel secure in your foundation? Why or why not?

This whole parable is referring to building the temple of God in us. Do you see how the layers of righteousness are all coming together? Righteousness is like an intricate piece of fabric woven together with every piece of thread lending to the building of the temple of God in us.

I don't know about you, but that's good news to us. That fills me with hope, joy, and peace knowing that I am firm in Him. Let's keep going! Open your Bible to Psalms and we'll wrap up this week's study.

> OPEN FOR ME THE GATES WHERE THE _____ ENTER, AND I WILL GO IN AND THANK THE LORD. THESE GATES LEAD TO THE PRESENCE OF THE LORD, AND THE GODLY ENTER THERE. I THANK YOU FOR ANSWERING MY PRAYER AND GIVING ME VICTORY! THE _____ THAT THE BUILDERS _____ HAS NOW BECOME THE _____. THIS IS THE LORD'S DOING, AND IT IS WONDERFUL TO SEE. THIS IS THE DAY THE LORD HAS MADE. WE WILL REJOICE AND BE GLAD IN IT.
> PSALM 118:19-24 NLT

Y'all may be shocked to learn the true meaning behind this verse. How long have we heard Psalm 118:24 and thought, Well, it's a new day that the Lord has made, I will rejoice and be glad in it?

We assumed this verse was referring to every day. Like, I'm alive, I should rejoice. Now that is true, we should always rejoice in a new day but that is not what this verse is referring to. Surprise, surprise. (We told you the reading through the Bible is like one big treasure hunt!!)

Did you notice what the Psalmist said first?

1. **"Open to me the gates of righteousness"**

The gates of righteousness were originally the gates of the temple which were opened to allow the worshipers to enter in. The righteousness of Jesus is what gives us access to BECOME the living temple of God almighty. Because of His righteousness we no longer have to enter the temple, we ARE the temple!

2. **He then says, "This is the gate of the LORD"**

Again, Jesus is our gate (John 10:9), He is our righteousness. He's the point of entry. Without Him, no one gets in. Jesus is the way, the truth, and the life and no one gets to the Father except through Him (John 14:6).

3. **"The righteous shall enter through"**

All who have accepted Jesus as their Savior shall enter through this gate. Amen!

4. **"I thank you that you have answered me and become my salvation. The stone that the builders rejected had become the cornerstone. This is the Lord's doing and it's marvelous in our eyes."**

Again, here is Jesus being displayed at the cornerstone of our faith.

5. **Now wait for it, here it comes . . .**

This is the day that the _____ has made; let us _____ and _____ in it. Psalm 118:24 NLT

Do you see it? THIS is the day, not just any day, but this specific day: The day we realize that it's because of our righteousness in Christ that we ARE the living, breathing temple of God Almighty—which is solely built on the foundation of Jesus—our cornerstone! Y'all this is life changing, kingdom-living, miracle-working, power-filled truth! This is a cause for a celebration! We need to rejoice and be glad in THIS!!! When our brothers and sisters in Christ understand this truth, it's then that they can begin to truly walk in the freedom of the Kingdom of God.

Isn't it so cool when the Word begins to unfold before our very own eyes?
This truly is something to rejoice in: The day we understand His righteousness is a good, good day.

SECRET PLACE Training

As you spend time in the secret place today we want to invite you to try something different, something that maybe you've never done with the Lord before and that's to celebrate. Celebrate all He's done, celebrate His goodness and His faithfulness, celebrate the righteousness of Jesus and the fact that you are covered in the fullness of Christ. So go for it, whatever celebrating looks like to you, do it, and invite your heavenly Father to join the festivities. Make a cake, blow some party whistles, pop some confetti, have fun with it.

Journaling

BREASTPLATE OF RIGHTEOUSNESS
THE PLUMB LINE
week five

Stand firm then with the belt of truth buckled around your waist with the breastplate of righteousness in place.

EPHESIANS 6:14

We've got to stay where? You've got to be kidding me. My eyes were as wide as saucers as my husband delivered the bad news. The camper we lived in full-time had just been assaulted by a falling hundred-year-old oak tree, which bent the frame and left a gaping hole in our home. Our insurance only reimbursed one week of stay in case of an emergency, but we needed a place to stay for months while we waited for the insurance's decision on whether to repair the damage or total the camper. We literally had nowhere else to stay (inexpensively) other than our damaged camper.

This was not a glamorous time of my life, and it was very humbling. The accident left our home-on-wheels off-kilter, despite our best efforts—which included some redneck solutions of jacking up the camper by our own devices—we could not get the camper level. This was during the dog days of summer, and if the air conditioning was not working, we would have sucked it up and forked over all the cash for a cool environment to temporarily crash . . . but since it worked we stuck it out.

I'm not sure if you've ever lived in a home that's not level, but let me give you a glimpse into what it's like. First and most noticeably, the toilets don't drain adequately. So there is a pungent stench and it requires a TON of effort to empty the tanks. Doors don't shut and locks don't lock properly. Your perception is off, and simple tasks like walking suddenly require much more focus, as you constantly strive to maintain your balance. You also trip . . . a lot. It's even hard to rest because you're wondering if you are going to in fact roll off the bed all night. So, to recap: Stank, not safe, open/unlocked doors (that you want closed/locked), off balance, trip easily, unrest. Yeah, not fun.

So, what does an unlevel camper with a hole in it have to do with the armor of God? Well, here is where it gets interesting. God obviously knew I would be writing this study and guess what He did? The Lord had me experience what happens when a house is "unlevel." Oh, I know the problems firsthand. Next, He showed me there a piece of the armor of God that ensures our "house" is level. Remember we are the house of the Holy Spirit, but if this one thing isn't in place—leveling our foundation, guess what will happen?

Things start to stink. The doors of our eyes, ears, and minds are left open to attack. It's hard to walk out our purpose. There is a lot of stumbling. And there is a lack of rest.

Well, this is not how the Lord wants us to live! Let's dig into the Word together and make sure we level-up our foundations so we can adequately armor up!

-Amber

THE PLUMB LINE

Scan for session five video

SESSION FIVE NOTES:

DAY ONE
righteous by faith

Before building a house, you must make sure the foundation is level. We've already been unpacking the verses in Ephesians six about the armor God that He wants us wearing, but this week we're talking about the revelation that sparked this whole study. Today, let's look at the words of Jesus in Mathew 6:33, fill in the blanks!

> SEEK _____ THE
> _____,
> AND _____ _____,
> AND ALL THESE THINGS WILL BE
> ADDED TO YOU.
> MATTHEW 6:33 ESV

When we read a verse we've read or heard a hundred times, it is easy to assume we know what it means. This one is usually interpreted as: Put God first. Now for clarity, we are completely in favor of putting God first in all things but is this verse really saying that? Let's look a bit closer. *Lord, reveal what Jesus is really saying here!* What two things are we supposed to seek?

1.

2.

Let's just look at those two words in the Greek.

RESEARCH MORE

KINGDOM is the Greek word: *basileia- kingdom, sovereignty, royal power* [5]

RESEARCH MORE

RIGHTEOUSNESS is the Greek word: *dikaiosuné- righteousness, justice, deemed right by the Lord, righteousness of which God is the source or author, but practically: a divine righteousness* [6]

When Jesus tells us to seek the Kingdom of God and His Righteousness He is saying: Find out about the royal power and authority of God and find out how to get right with God—His way! He also communicated how important it is to find this out "first." And all the other things build from that. Now you may be wondering why we're spending weeks unpacking righteousness, it is because this foundation needs to be set in order for everything else to work!

The great thing is we've already talked about how to get right with God through faith . . . but since this may be a newer concept to some, we've got some more verses to prove it. Fill in the blanks from these verses in Romans:

> FOR I AM NOT ASHAMED OF THE _____, FOR IT IS THE _____ OF GOD FOR SALVATION TO EVERYONE WHO _____, TO THE JEW FIRST AND ALSO TO THE GREEK. FOR IN IT THE _____ IS REVEALED FROM FAITH TO FAITH; AS IT IS WRITTEN, "BUT THE RIGHTEOUS MAN SHALL LIVE BY FAITH."
> ROMANS 1:16-17 NASB

According to this passage, what does the gospel reveal?

Does the righteousness of God come by works, or does it say faith?

Now, did you notice that understanding this truth is the "power" of God for salvation (deliverance) to anyone who "believes." It's about believing in what Jesus did, not doing something to earn salvation or righteousness. Let this sink in . . . God is not looking at your actions, He is looking at what your faith is in. Is your faith in Jesus? I know, I know, we already covered this, but we just want to be sure your heart has embraced the truth of it all. This is where we must start, because this is what Jesus told us to do first.

Find out about the power to deliver you (Kingdom), discover the way to get right with God (Righteousness) . . . then every other marvelous truth and breakthrough can begin. Again, we're just making sure the breastplate of righteousness is fitted firm and secure.

Have you ever read the scripture from Matthew 6:33 and assumed it meant "put God first"?

Do you feel there is a deeper meaning?

What is God showing you?

Spend some time asking the Lord to reveal what this verse is really about and how it applies to you.

Journaling

Journaling

DAY TWO
righteousness is the plumb line

I cannot believe the pieces of the armor of God are hidden in the Old Testament book of Zechariah!! In the video sessions, we talk about how the book of Zechariah documents the words and instructions from God about how to rebuild the physical temple, and as we read through it, we noticed pieces of the armor. Don't miss the significance, because in the New Testament, we are the temple of God, so things mentioned in the rebuilding of the physical temple absolutely correlate with the building up of the spiritual temple within us! Today, we're going to talk about where righteousness is mentioned in Zechariah and the scripture which inspired this whole study!

The following scripture is one of the most quoted verses from Zechariah, but it's usually only referenced "in part", so in true Amber and Dianne fashion we will be unpacking the whole verse, and it is SO exciting! So, let's jump in and see what it's all about—you know the drill, fill in the blanks!

> DO NOT DESPISE THESE SMALL _____, FOR THE LORD REJOICES TO SEE THE WORK _____, TO SEE THE _____ IN ZERUBBABEL'S HAND.
> ZECHARIAH 4:10 NLT

This verse is often used to encourage someone who is just starting, or the importance of humble beginnings, you know: don't get discouraged because it looks small. But guess what we found out?! This is actually hiding a deeper meaning! Did you notice "begin" is mentioned twice? We found out this scripture is really saying, to build the temple accurately you have to begin here. Begin where? This is where it gets good!!!

What is in Zerubbabel's hand?

Well, in order to get a full picture we're going to need to find out where the plumb line is explained, and low and behold . . .

Armor Up

Isaiah defines it! Fill in the blanks y'all!

> AND I WILL MAKE JUSTICE THE LINE, AND _____ THE PLUMB LINE;
> ISAIAH 28:17 ESV

What is the plumb line y'all (according to Isaiah)?

Also in antiquity, the plumb line is the tool used to "level" the house. It is what makes sure the foundation is correctly leveled. So essentially this verse is saying it is God's righteousness that levels our house.

Okay, okay, but who is Zerubbabel? Well, he represents a few things! One, he was actually the governor of Judah at the time this book of the Bible was written, who was enthusiastic about and was overseeing the rebuilding of the temple. Two, he was also a foreshadow of Jesus, because Jesus is passionate about and builds His church. Three, we also found out he is actually in the lineage of Jesus, one of His ancestors. So amazing! Four, Zerubbabel can also represent those who are passionate about ensuring the people of God are being built correctly, on the right foundation!

Okay so let's put all this information together!

We believe the Lord was really saying: Do not look down on this seemingly insignificant, small start, for the LORD rejoices to see the work beginning on the right, secure, level foundation, to see righteousness in Jesus' hand, to see His church grasping His righteousness!

Our righteousness is first and foremost in the hands of Jesus, not ourselves! Praise God! Secondly, the Lord rejoices when we grasp this fact! This is the beginning of having a level foundation! When we've "got a hold" of His righteousness that . . .

comes through faith in Jesus, y'all God is rejoicing! This isn't small and shouldn't be looked down on, this is actually the starting point of a secure foundation! Our heavenly Father is so happy when we open His gift of righteousness to us! We are right with God because of Jesus! It's in His hands, not ours! It was up to Him, not us!!! This is something to celebrate! Which is why we unpacked the meaning behind Psalm 118:24 last week and its connection to understanding this! THIS is the day the Lord has made (the day we'd grasp righteousness, and understand what His Son did for us!), we will rejoice and be glad in it!!

His righteousness is the plumb line—it's what keeps you plumb, built up straight on the cornerstone which is Jesus. He is the absolute, the only way to have right standing before God. Because of God's grace we now have the privilege to stand right before God. This is so so good! That's why the gospel is called the "good news."

If our house is not leveled in His righteousness, it is often based on our own righteousness. This is how the Pharisees lived and it causes all kinds of problems. Our righteousness is a bad plumb line because our obedience can never be consistent. Guess whose behavior was? Jesus. Think of the story of the unlevel camper. If we're built on our righteousness, everything is off: rotten stench, open to attack, tripping, out of balance, in this type of self-righteous spiritual house there is a hierarchy mentality, judgmental, fear . . . so many problems! Our house must be leveled by God's righteousness, not ours!!

When we grasp this, boy that breastplate of righteousness is getting more and more secure! It's never going to be secure when it is based on our works because it would be falling off every time we didn't act good enough. However, when that piece of armor stays fastened because it's based on Jesus' work, we understand, *wow, it's never coming off*. I'm always going to be counted righteous because of Jesus. Place faith in His work and put the plumb line in your hand: Breastplate of righteousness secured!

SECRET PLACE Training

The breastplate of righteousness has often been presented that it means you need to act right to be protected. But the righteousness of God has never been about you at all, but instead about Jesus! Notice the phrase "righteousness of God" does not say the "righteousness of you". Haha. Seriously though, this righteousness is God's and it is given to you to wear as a gift.

Ask the Lord: *Have I been clinging to a righteousness (being right with God) that is up to me? In my mind, has it been in my hands to accomplish?*

Write down what He reveals.

Now ask Him: *Teach me how to grasp your righteousness! Help me to see that being right with you is really and has always been in Jesus' hands. Level my house Lord and put me on the right foundation so I can walk in victory and authority!*

Journaling

DAY THREE
starting to act righteous

We want to open up every gift God has for us, am I right? Yesterday, we talked about where our lives and spiritual houses must begin. Our plumb line must be Jesus and His righteousness, or everything will be off. Well, the writers of the book of Hebrews takes it even further, declaring that we can't even grow if we don't get a hold of this! Read the following verses in Hebrews five and six and see what you discover!

> IN FACT, THOUGH BY THIS TIME YOU OUGHT TO BE TEACHERS, YOU NEED SOMEONE TO TEACH YOU THE _____ TRUTHS OF GOD'S WORD ALL OVER AGAIN. YOU NEED MILK, NOT SOLID FOOD! ANYONE WHO LIVES ON _____, BEING STILL AN _____, IS NOT ACQUAINTED WITH THE TEACHING ABOUT _____ BUT SOLID FOOD IS FOR THE MATURE, WHO BY CONSTANT USE HAVE TRAINED THEMSELVES TO DISTINGUISH GOOD FROM EVIL. THEREFORE, HAVING LEFT THE . . .

> _____ TEACHING OF THE CHRIST, WE SHOULD GO ON TO MATURITY, NOT LAYING AGAIN A _____ OF REPENTANCE FROM DEAD _____, AND FAITH IN GOD . . .
> HEBREWS 5:12-14 NIV
> & HEBREWS 6:1 BSB

Did you get that, "anyone who lives on milk, being still an infant is not acquainted with the teachings of" what?

If we haven't learned because of Jesus we've been made righteous by faith not action, we can't grow. We have to understand the "elementary teachings of Christ" before we can go to spiritual Middle, High school, College teachings . . . ultimately to grow in the Lord, we must have the correct foundation—otherwise we stay immature! Well, we don't want that!

It says "solid food is for the"?

Remember Dianne's vision with a wall separating her from all the gifts and good things God had for her? Everything on that table was the "solid food" and she began to open all God had for as she learned the teaching of righteousness by faith in Christ. Understanding this is when we start getting fed solid foods and start living on the other side of the wall—that's when "all these things will be added to you."

The Word of God is so beautiful, it's woven together so intricately. Can you see how all of these truths are built on Jesus, our cornerstone? He is literally the Rock of Salvation. Our saving and growth depends on Him and we're unpacking this further when we discuss the helmet of salvation!

This may seem crazy but it's an interesting parallel. Think about the differences between an infant and a adult.

Why is it so important for Christians to get past the infant stage?

In the Hebrew passage we've been looking at, it mentions a shift in our foundation right at the end. We go from dead works (which don't save anyone!) and to faith in?

Faith in God instead of faith in our works. It is a complete mindset change—which is what repent means! Switch from thinking it's about you and your work and realize it's about the work of Jesus! The word repentance was used regularly in ancient Greek society and it literally means a change in mind:

In Greek the word for repentance means: *metanoia: change of mind, repent* [7]

RESEARCH MORE

This word in the original language actually means: Change the way you think! (Which will affect the way you act, by the way.) You can literally substitute "change your mind" every time you see repent because this is what it means.

The basis of our relationship with God really hinges on our understanding of His righteousness. We want to point out that even though we've been made righteous, it does not automatically make everything we do righteous. We are still going to mess up, but as we recognize what Jesus has truly done we begin to flourish in our relationship with Him, then our heart, thoughts, and actions begin to reflect more and more of Him. Beholding Jesus, makes us walk like Jesus! Grasping what He's done for us, causes us to act more like Him and less like our old nature!

SECRET PLACE Training

Open your Bible to Romans 4:5 and write it below (keeping in mind justified means declared righteous):

Pray and ask God to reveal what this means to you. *Lord, am I trusting in my works—behavior, obedience, ticking all the good Christian boxes—to be justified in your sight? Or am I believing you took care of this for me through your Son, Jesus. Reveal where my faith truly is. Show me how You really see me.*

Write down what you feel God reveals:

Journaling

DAY FOUR
righteousness produces boldness

A level foundation ABSOLUTELY matters. A structure can't be built properly or function correctly without level groundwork. We've learned this week the great level-er of our foundation, as the temple of the Holy Spirit, is understanding Jesus' sacrifice imputed righteousness to any who would believe in Him! This is the beginning! We must start and build from there.

Knowing this begins to lift the weight of shame and perfection off our shoulders, and automatically begins transforming us into the image of Christ! When we're wearing His righteousness (not ours) like a banner, we glorify Him and we begin acting like Him! Not only that, but understanding what Jesus did gives us the confidence to start sharing the gospel like never before. It is like opening the most amazing gift and you cannot wait to tell other people. Being established in His righteousness not only levels our spiritual house, changes our mind from earning to receiving this gracious gift, puts us on solid ground, but it also gives us a boldness we've never had and a peace we've never known!

Look up these scriptures and fill in the blanks:

> THE WICKED FLEE THOUGH NO ONE PURSUES, BUT THE _____ ARE AS _____ AS A LION.
> PROVERBS 28:1 NIV

What attribute describes someone who knows they are righteous?

For years, I struggled with confidence. I would pray to be bolder in my witness, but it seemed so unattainable. Turns out I didn't need a confidence boost; I needed a revelation of righteousness by faith! When I got that, oh I was witnessing to everyone! I finally understood and had some good news to share! Boldness is a direct result of recognizing we are declared righteous by faith in Jesus.

Do you feel that having a better understanding of righteousness has increased your boldness in sharing the gospel?

If so, make it your goal to share the gospel with one person this week and share your experience with a close friend!

Now look at this:

> IN _____ YOU WILL BE _____: _____ WILL BE FAR FROM YOU; YOU WILL HAVE NOTHING TO _____. _____ WILL BE FAR REMOVED; IT WILL NOT COME NEAR YOU.
> ISAIAH 54:14 NIV

What must we be established in?

Look at the definition of *established-* **accepted and recognized, successful, growing and flourishing.**[8]

Well, isn't this interesting?! Pair the definition with the verse from Isaiah—and all that we've been learning—and we see something HUGE. Accepting and recognizing the righteousness of God, He has gifted to us, helps us successfully live the Christian life and sets us up to grow and flourish! This is why it's the plumb line, why we must be founded on the cornerstone of Jesus Christ. His work, not ours! Because being established in righteousness is what sets us up for victory!!!! But that is not all. Once we're established and thriving what are gaining victory over? What does the verse list?

1.

2.

3.

When we think we are righteous by works or behavior, it is actually oppressive and tyrannical, and causes worry, fear, even terror. We can be overcome by these things if we don't know who we are in Christ and what we have in Him! But notice the anecdote is not a surge of bravery or doing more for God. No! The solution is accepting His righteousness!!! When we are founded on truth, that we're right with God by believing in Jesus we become overcomers in Christ!

Let's wrap up this day with confirmation on all we've learned today by taking one more look at Romans chapter five. Fill in the missing words!

> FOR THE SIN OF THIS ONE MAN, ADAM, CAUSED DEATH TO RULE OVER MANY. BUT EVEN GREATER IS GOD'S WONDERFUL _____ AND HIS GIFT OF _____, FOR ALL WHO _____ IT WILL LIVE IN _____ OVER SIN AND DEATH THROUGH THIS ONE MAN, JESUS CHRIST.
> ROMANS 5:17 NLT

This is a powerful promise! Again, we see being right with God is a gift He gives we cannot earn it. We also see that what Jesus did is greater than what Adam did! Adam's disobedience caused everyone after him to be ruled by death. But Jesus came and changed that and whoever received the gracious gift of God would not be ruled by death but instead would live in what?

So, accepting His righteousness and living through the strength of Christ causes us to have victory over sin and death! This is incredible! But the gift has to be accepted and received! This means we must take a hold of this truth and walk in it. This whole series is about winning the battles of life and walking in victory, but without an understanding of the righteousness of God, can you see how that is impossible? But with the breastplate of righteousness in place we can take on the strongest enemy!

SECRET PLACE Training

Today, we learned what laying a hold of "righteous by faith" produces in our life: boldness, freedom from fear, terror, and oppression, victory over sin and death. Of the few things mentioned, which one do you need the most breakthrough in?

Say a simple prayer and ask the Father how this area relates to righteousness. Ask Him to truly establish you in righteousness and for Him to teach you how to live and flourish from this place.

Journaling

BREASTPLATE OF RIGHTEOUSNESS
ROBE OF ROYALTY

week six

Stand firm then with the belt of truth buckled around your waist with the breastplate of righteousness in place.

EPHESIANS 6:14

There once was a young, orphaned girl living in a country not her own. She was an exiled, immigrant with no real significance. As an orphan and a female, she had no inheritance. As an outcast, belonging to a people captured in war—her life didn't mean much in that society. But God had quite an unexpected plan for this little one.

The young girl grew in favor with all she met and became beautiful inside and out. Then the unexpected happened! The King was determined to find a wife to rule at his side, and this young woman was chosen as a candidate. She excelled above the others, despite her humble beginnings and eventually won the heart of the King of the biggest territory on earth. If you haven't guessed it yet, we're not talking about Cinderella, this is the true story of Queen Esther!

Now, Esther went from exile to a queen! This was a whole new world to her and she had to learn how to act like royalty, talk like royalty, and command others like royalty. She had a few things to unlearn from her old mentality and a whole lot more to learn about her new position of power! Our good friend Melissa Mendez, owner of Embracing Royal Beauty, always says, "Esther went from being an exiled orphan to favored queen. I would say her process of purification and refinement also meant mindset shifts to overcome any insecurities so she could step into who she was meant to be and live it out with authority."

In a lot of ways, Queen Esther's journey from pauper to royalty mirrors the church. We start out not knowing our heavenly Father, being exiled in a world that has fallen very far from the Garden of Eden God had created for humanity. But suddenly we meet the King of kings, we meet Jesus, and we put our faith in Him and the two become one. Now we're the Bride of Christ and sometimes, we don't know how to act royal!

We perhaps still have old, condemning, orphan/outcast mindsets that make us think: No one really loves me, I don't belong, I'm not included, I'm insignificant. Don't you think there were days Esther thought these things?

But she had to remember that was her old self, she was a completely new person because of her marriage to the King. She didn't do anything to get this new position, it was a gift! She became queen because the King wanted her, and it's just the same for us. God wanted us, so He sent Jesus to reunite us to Himself!

In Christ, we have a new position! We must learn to see ourselves through the lens of our union with Jesus. Because of Him we are considered the royal children of God and the Bride of Christ! At a wedding ceremony, a couple exchanges rings, and when we were united with Christ, He gave us a spiritual ring, so to speak, representing Jesus giving us His authority!

Because we are one with Christ we have access to all of Heaven. He wants us to use His authority to bring change on the earth! Just as Queen Esther used her new royal position to save her people, God is calling his sons and daughters to step up, speak out, and walk in His authority to bring the people of the world the good news of the salvation of Jesus!

When we understand we are clothed in His righteousness, we begin walking in our authority! We aren't who we used to be, we've become royalty! Now let's walk like we are!

ROBE OF ROYALTY

Scan for session six video

SESSION SIX NOTES:

DAY ONE
abiding in Christ

Okay, let's get practical! We've covered a lot of ground here on the topic of righteousness, but what does it look like to play this whole thing out in everyday life? What do we do when we don't feel like we are covered in the righteousness of Christ Jesus? What do we do when we mess up and lose our temper or make decisions that are less than our best? This is when the real battle begins. This is where you must make a decision, where are you choosing to stand? Are you going to stand on the firm foundation of Jesus and His truth or are you going to choose to stand on the sifting sand of your own righteousness? Let's look back at what Jesus says about a wise person in Matthew chapter seven, fill in the blanks.

> "THEREFORE EVERYONE WHO HEARS THESE WORDS OF MINE AND PUTS THEM INTO PRACTICE IS LIKE A _____ MAN WHO BUILT HIS HOUSE ON THE _____. THE RAIN CAME DOWN, THE STREAMS ROSE, AND THE WINDS BLEW AND BEAT AGAINST THAT HOUSE; YET IT DID NOT FALL, BECAUSE IT HAD ITS _____ ON THE _____ . . .

> BUT EVERYONE WHO HEARS THESE WORDS OF MINE AND DOES NOT PUT THEM INTO PRACTICE IS LIKE A _____ MAN WHO BUILT HIS HOUSE ON _____. THE RAIN CAME DOWN, THE STREAMS ROSE, AND THE WINDS BLEW AND BEAT AGAINST THAT HOUSE, AND IT _____ WITH A GREAT CRASH."
> MATTHEW 7:24-27 NIV

We know the wise person built on the rock (Jesus), but what does the foolish person build on?

What happens to the home built on the sand?

We must stand secure in who we are in Christ—no matter what comes our way, or we're going to crumble! It seems so complicated in the moment, but the reality is no matter what we think, we are who God says we are. So, what do we do when we fall short, when we go through the storms of life and are depleted and stumbling?

We pick ourselves up, dust ourselves off, and remember who we are in Christ, declaring: "I am the righteousness of God through Christ Jesus! I may not be perfect, but Jesus is." Then we apologize to the Lord for not acting in alignment with our true selves and ask Him to help us next time. We can't let our mistakes define us, we must let God's Word define us!

Just like in any arena in life, we learn from our mistakes. With that being said, take inventory of yourself. What triggers you, what tempts you, what entices you? Then, make a plan to distance yourself, minimize your exposure to those things, or bring light to the darkness. Be open and honest with a trusted friend, see a counselor, set healthy boundaries, openly communicate your feelings, declare the Word over your situation, etc . . . learn and grow. For example, if you struggle with your worth, memorize Romans 8:1 and declare that truth over yourself daily until it sinks into your head and heart.

> THERE IS NOW NO _____ FOR THOSE WHO ARE IN _____.
> ROMANS 8:1 NIV

Come on, that scripture should make you shout!

Maybe this illustration will help. Let's take it back to Noah and the ark. Imagine the ark is representing Jesus—the vessel that "saved" Noah and his whole family. They were hidden safe inside the ark during the flood. Now, envision the winds raging and the rain crashing down causing Noah to trip and fall. But get this, he was still inside the ark. Even though he perhaps stumbled, Noah didn't fall off the vessel, he was still inside the boat. It's no different than us. Sometimes the storms of life may cause us to trip or fall, but we must remember Who it is that we are in, as believers we are still "in Christ." This scripture proves it.

> FOR THOUGH THE RIGHTEOUS FALL SEVEN TIMES, THEY RISE AGAIN, BUT THE WICKED STUMBLE WHEN CALAMITY STRIKES.
> PROVERBS 24:16 NIV

Does it say the righteous don't fall?

No! It says "though they fall", and it's not just once! It's several times, but what happens next? THEY RISE!! Why is that? Because their foundation is Jesus. The storm came, but their house didn't blow down because they had a sure foundation! Sometimes we may think a righteous person won't fall, but the Bible says otherwise!

How can a person who falls still be called righteous? Because their righteousness is not based on themselves! They are getting that label because of someone else's work: Jesus the Christ.

Now look at what happens to wicked when calamity strikes. They stumble and there is no report of them rising. Their foundation was themself.

After all of the scriptures we've worked through over the last few weeks, I think we can agree that our behavior is NOT what made us righteous. If that's true—which it is—then why would we think that our behavior can make us unrighteous? Our righteousness has NEVER been about our behavior, but Christ's.

Again, this isn't a free pass to sin. If that's what you're thinking, then you're missing the point. It's about our identity and our relationship with Jesus. When we have a relationship with Him and we understand what it is that He's really done for us, we don't want to sin, it's a relationship built on love, respect, honor, and trust.

> "_____ IN ME, AND I IN YOU. AS THE BRANCH CANNOT BEAR FRUIT BY ITSELF, UNLESS . . .
> IT _____ IN THE VINE, NEITHER CAN YOU, UNLESS YOU _____ IN ME."
> JOHN 15:4 ESV

We can only produce fruit when we what?

Are you wondering what the fruit is? We can learn about it in Galatians so let's take a look.

> BUT THE _____ OF THE _____ IS LOVE, JOY, PEACE, PATIENCE, KINDNESS, GOODNESS, FAITHFULNESS, GENTLENESS, SELF-CONTROL: AGAINST SUCH THINGS THERE IS NO LAW.
> GALATIANS 5: 22-23 ESV

Here it is again. Notice when we abide in Christ we become equipped to do the impossible.

> "IF YOU _____ IN ME, AND MY WORDS _____ IN YOU, ASK WHATEVER YOU WISH, AND IT WILL BE DONE FOR YOU."
> JOHN 15:7 ESV

Let's touch base really quick on what it actually means to abide in someone or something. It basically means to accept, to remain, or stay.

So do you see what's happening? We are the righteousness of God through Christ Jesus. And when we choose to abide in Him, to stay in His covering, to accept this truth of our new identity, and remain in Him, then we will reap the benefits of that decision. We'll experience the fruit of the Spirit, our prayers will hold power, and like the story of Noah above, we'll walk in peace and confidence because we know Who it is that we are in. At the onset of this study we said: The armor of God is really Jesus. Abiding in Jesus is really abiding in the armor, this is how we stay Armored Up, by living each day in the revelation of who we really are in Him.

Journaling

SECRET PLACE Training

How did the Noah illustration settle with you? Did it make you uncomfortable or bring relief to think that you are still in Christ, even if you mess up? If it made you uncomfortable, ask the Lord to reveal to you what caused the discomfort and ask Him to replace it with joy.

Take some time today to read through John 15:1-17 write down all that God has available for you to walk in when you abide in Christ. List at least five things that are available to you when you understand you live in Christ and Christ lives in you.

Journaling

Journaling

DAY TWO
the death, life, and resurrection

Freedom produces joy! Recently we watched a clip of a woman being freed from prison in another country after being wrongfully accused. We could sense the joy in her eyes as she tasted freedom once more! We could literally feel her emotions through the screen—her delight, gratitude, and excitement all shown through her sparkling eyes, beaming smile, and mannerisms. She was filled with pure joy, relief, and comfort because she was now set free. Y'all, this is us, except we haven't been wrongfully accused. We were rightfully accused, but the love of God was greater. He made a way to not only rescue us and free us, but to redeem us. He made a way to make us new. Jesus stepped in and took what we deserved and just like this woman we have a newfound freedom available for us to walk in. How exciting is this?!

We no longer have to stay confined, fearful, and afraid. We don't have to stay stuck in the self-sabotaging rhythms of the life we once knew. We no longer have to live in defeat and condemnation because we know the Word of God. Again, it has nothing to do with our works, but everything to do with the finished work of Jesus. His life, death, and resurrection. I know it's been said like a thousand times, but it's critical we get this! Write the missing words of the following well-known scripture.

> "THEN YOU WILL KNOW THE _____, AND THE _____ WILL SET YOU FREE."
> JOHN 8:32 NIV

Y'all, every lie spoken over us is a seed of the enemy trying to make its way into the soil of our souls. Do not let it germinate! Get it out, it's the truth that sets us free. The lies keep us captive.

It's imperative that we know what the Bible says so we can stand firm against the enemy.

This is what the whole armor is about. So the very next time the enemy makes you feel less than your best, declare truth over those feelings and thoughts and take authority over the lies being thrown at you. Jesus has already forgiven you of your sins. He died and took them to the grave and left them there. You truly are free!

Look at the next scripture to help this really sink in. So often the religious teach that the work of Jesus stopped at the cross, but if we keep reading we see that it actually continues through resurrection, and in the book of Revelation we find out He is still at work! Jesus didn't just die for our sins, He also rose to make us right with God. Take a look at this and fill in what is missing:

> HE WAS HANDED OVER TO _____ BECAUSE OF OUR SINS, AND HE WAS _____ TO LIFE TO MAKE US _____ WITH GOD.
> ROMANS 4:25 NLT

When Jesus was raised to life, what did that make us?

If we stop at the cross, the sins are taken away, but we're still not righteous.

We have to look at the work of the cross, but then also understand what happened next! Jesus isn't dead, He's alive and because He defeated the grave we have the ability to be right with God! *Praise Jesus!*

If we haven't hit the ball out of the park yet on the breastplate of righteousness, let us say it this way: Your identity is no longer sinner, it's saint! Picture this label plastered across your armor! Let's start living this truth out. Can you imagine if we all walked around knowing our true identity? Jesus died to make *you* holy, to make *you* righteous, to make *you* a child of God and the Bride of Christ!! It's *His* blood, *His* death, and *His* resurrection that makes you who you are. You are the righteousness of God through Christ Jesus. (2 Corinthians 5:21) *Amen!* Are you fired up yet? I don't know about y'all but we're ready to take some ground for the Kingdom of God! We've got the best news to share!

SECRET PLACE Training

List some attributes of the royal family. What do they have access to that commoners don't?

Now compare that list of commodities with those available in the Kingdom of God. Do you notice a lot of similarities? In what areas are you lacking and how can you step fully into that area and live as the royalty that you are?

Spend some time sharing your heart with your Heavenly Father on this matter. Ask Him to give you a royal mindset!

Journaling

DAY THREE
we are royalty

Imagine you have been born into the most royal family ever. Shut your eyes for a moment and actually visualize this. Picture what your environment would be, what would you wear, how would you walk and talk? What would your attitude be? Would you carry yourself differently, would your head be held up with confidence—walking with your shoulders back a bit? Would you think differently, expect different? Would you live and act differently than you do now?

Let's take it even further, because you are a part of this royal family, you now have access to everything that the royal family has. Everything they have is available to you. It's at your disposal. Knowing that, wouldn't you want to share the provision, favor, and protection? Wouldn't you want to use the abundant finances to be a financial blessing to those in need? If all the royal power is available to you, how would you help your friends and family? Wouldn't you want to make a difference in your community, your cities, and the nations?

The reality is we are part of the royal . . . family, as children of God—we are the Bride of Jesus Christ *the* King of kings. We need to step up and into the royalty that is available to us. Let's look at what the Bible says about our new royal position, fill in the blanks:

> BUT YOU ARE A _____ PEOPLE, A _____ PRIESTHOOD, A _____ NATION, GOD'S _____ POSSESSION, THAT YOU MAY DECLARE THE PRAISES OF HIM WHO CALLED YOU OUT OF DARKNESS INTO HIS WONDERFUL LIGHT.
> 1 PETER 2:9 NIV

We are called:
_____ people
_____ priesthood
_____ nation
God's _____ possession.

How are you feeling about God describing you with these words? Why is that?

Are you beginning to see that we are very significant to God? As a part of the royal, special family, we have to understand who we are and what we have access to! The shepherd boy David knew who he was and knew he was equipped by God when he went into battle and defeated Goliath. So we too must understand who we are and what it is that God has equipped us to *be* and *do* and then *go* and *do* it.

Don't stay locked outside the gates of the Kingdom when you hold the keys! You are royalty and you have a palace with your name on it. Go slay your giant, go take back your land! Chase down your promises, step into your calling and live out the royal version of you that you are.

Maybe you're reading through this and thinking: Yeah, but what does that look like in real life?

- It looks like discovering and standing on the promises of God! (Which by the way there are a WHOLE lot of promises for the "righteous" throughout the Bible—look through Proverbs! Maybe, like us, you didn't know that applied to you, because you haven't been good enough? Now, we know better! We're righteous because Jesus was good enough and gifted it to us! All the promises of God are yes and amen "in Christ!" 2 Corinthians 1:20)

- It looks like taking the sword of the Spirit, the Word of God and believing it to be true for you!

- It looks like believing that you are a child of God! So walk in the will of your Father.

Lift your voice, declare the truth of God's word over yourself, and understand the power of your prayers because . . .

THE PRAYER OF A _____ PERSON IS _____ AND _____.
JAMES 5:16B NIV

Did you catch the prerequisite? When you understand that you are the righteousness of God through Christ Jesus, your prayers become powerful and effective. Your voice carries life, truth, and victory for the Kingdom! *Amen!*

Do you tend to see yourself through a prince or pauper mentality? Why is this?

Jesus was the King of all the earth, but He was also the most humble to ever walk it. Royal doesn't mean prideful or cocky, it is a position of humble authority, knowing who we really are in the LORD. The best Kings and leaders serve others! Spend some time with your Heavenly Father and ask Him to give you a royal perspective of yourself.

Journaling

DAY FOUR
robe of righteousness

We know you are sad to hear this is the last day on the breastplate of righteousness. Haha! Yes, it's true the weeks of fire are coming to a close. But we must tell you why we've spent so many weeks unpacking this subject. Because for years we thought you had to consistently "do" good enough to "be" considered right with God. We were confused about the gospel! We basically thought Jesus made a way for us to be righteous, but it was up to us to achieve it. We didn't realize HE WAS THE WAY. Then we found out that Jesus is our righteousness, and our minds were BLOWN! The whole time it was a righteousness that comes by faith!! We haven't stopped talking about it since! We thought perhaps some of those doing the study might have thought the same? We wanted to let it marinate for a few weeks.

To bring this whole piece of the armor home, and how righteousness is tied to our royalty, and why this is important, look up Isaiah sixty-one and complete the following sentences!

I DELIGHT GREATLY IN THE LORD; MY SOUL REJOICES IN MY GOD. FOR HE HAS _____ ME WITH GARMENTS OF _____ AND ARRAYED ME IN A _____ OF _____, AS A BRIDEGROOM ADORNS HIS HEAD LIKE A PRIEST, AND AS A _____ ADORNS HERSELF WITH HER JEWELS. FOR AS THE SOIL MAKES THE SPROUT COME UP AND A GARDEN CAUSES SEEDS TO GROW, SO THE SOVEREIGN LORD WILL MAKE _____ AND _____ SPRING UP BEFORE ALL NATIONS.
ISAIAH 61:10-11 NIV

God has clothed us in the garments of?

HE HAS ARRAYED US IN A _____ OF _____.

Are we clothed in His righteousness or ours?

Right, and did we put it on or did He?

Again as if we needed reminding, but we're going to highlight it anyway; God did it for us! He put a robe of His righteousness on us!

The word "robe" needs some attention. **In Hebrew it is the word *meil*: robe, cloak, coat, mantle.**[9] This was a robe worn by men of rank, worn by the daughters of David, or a robe of high priest. Not just anyone wore a robe. The royals, the highest in God's temple, and the people who had authority.

We hope you are starting to see that not only is the breastplate of righteousness protective, it is also declarative of your identity. God has literally given us a royal robe and with that comes power, authority, a position in the Kingdom of heaven. He's put His righteousness on us and commissioned us to walk in His Kingdom power to exercise His will on the earth. This has always been His plan. Let's take a look at the first blessing over man and woman found in the book of Genesis. Take a look at Genesis one.

> AND GOD _____ THEM [GRANTING THEM CERTAIN AUTHORITY] AND SAID TO THEM, "BE FRUITFUL, MULTIPLY, AND FILL THE EARTH, AND _____ IT [PUTTING IT UNDER YOUR POWER]; AND RULE OVER (DOMINATE) THE FISH OF THE SEA, THE BIRDS OF THE AIR, AND EVERY LIVING THING THAT MOVES UPON THE EARTH."
> GENESIS 1:28 AMP

God granted them what?

Was this just given to Adam or was it to male and female?

When God created humanity, He blessed male and female with authority to rule over the earth *together*. When the fall of mankind happened, they forfeited their power, but God had a plan! Through Christ, our authority has been restored! Jesus took back the dominion of the earth from the enemy and He gave His followers the keys to His Kingdom and made us His representatives to exercise His will! When He put His robe of authority and righteousness on us, He commissioned us to walk in His ways and work out His will for the earth! We are co-heirs and co-laborers with Christ!

Wearing the breastplate of righteousness is having an awareness of our royal position before the Father and taking our place in His Kingdom as His ambassadors! The enemy wants us constantly questioning if we are right with God so we stay stuck in a holding pattern of insecurity and never take back what he has stolen! We say NO MORE! God wants us to know that the gospel reveals Jesus made us right with God and our part is to believe it, then walk in our authority! Let's advance forward triumphantly with the breastplate of righteousness firmly fastened!

SECRET PLACE TRAINING

Write down your favorite version of Isaiah 61:10 and commit it to memory. Any time you question if you are right with God, quote it and remember: He put the robe of righteousness on you through Jesus! You had nothing to do with it, other than just believing in your Savior!

Journaling

SHOES FITTED WITH THE GOSPEL OF PEACE
week seven

As shoes for your feet having put on the readiness given by the gospel of peace.

EPHESIANS 6:15

Peace? Not real riveting. I was less than thrilled when the Lord gave me this word for the year, back in 2022. I was hoping for "breakthrough", "warrior", "resilient" or something more spectacular and flashy, but peace? *Boring.* Or so I incorrectly thought. Isn't God gracious to put up with and love us through our foolishness? Even though I wasn't wowed, God knew what I needed more than I did.

Little did I know what the year would hold—it turned out to be the most tumultuous year of our life! Not only was I running a household, full-time wifing, and momming (are these words? I feel they should be!), but I was also releasing two books and hosting an annual women's conference . . . all of this while living in a camper full-time. You can guess what happened—as I shared some of my journey during the plumb line week of living in an unlevel camper—but just so we can relive the moment together, I'll recap the disaster!

God will keep you safe during the storm! My husband and I were the camp pastors at a local summer camp and this particular day we felt compelled to preach a message on His protection during storms.

We had never preached a sermon on this topic before, but we knew we had to, didn't know why, but God did. That VERY afternoon a microburst storm popped up out of nowhere with tornado-magnitude winds, lightning and thunder like you couldn't believe! I was glued to the window watching all that was unfolding. Suddenly the ground began to move, it was pulsing from the weight of the tree that was about to topple over and the roots were pressing up against the soil. We watched in horror as this massive oak tree pummeled our brand new camper.

I'm going to take this moment right here to believe God still speaks to people. Ten minutes before the disaster, I was in my camper, and our new puppy was sleeping below it outside. My husband felt the Lord say "Call Amber and tell her to get out of the camper, and get the dog." I thought it would be fine, but trusted my husband's ability to hear from the Lord. I quickly grabbed our puppy, ran to higher and more secure ground. Minutes later the camper was ruined. I shutter to think what would have happened if I doubted my husband. So yeah, God still speaks and I am alive to testify about it!

After this, we had to scramble to find a place to live while we waited for the verdict from insurance, which was not a short process. All of our local family was housing other people in need, so as you guys already know, for a few weeks we stayed in the unlevel camper in the craziest of conditions! To say I was struggling to find peace would be a massive understatement. I didn't know where we were going to live and how we'd pay all the new bills we acquired because of the disaster! I remember hopelessly sitting with the Lord one morning bawling my eyes out at the state of our life, it felt everything but abundant.

It was then, when my circumstances were dire, God reminded me of one little verse: Seek first the Kingdom of God and His righteousness and all these things will be added to you as well (Matthew 6:33). I knew what to do! I marched in to Andrew and declared, "We might not know how this is going to work out. We might be living in a very crappy situation. We don't know where we are going to lay our head tomorrow. But we do know what we need to do! Seek God's Kingdom! We need to seek the peace of God right now! We need to pray and ask for His Kingdom to invade our situation before one thing changes!"

Andrew was in agreement. We stopped everything and prayed, asking the Lord to flood our hearts and home with His peace . . .

And guess what? He actually did! Suddenly we had this unexplainable peace. Trust in God replaced the worry in our hearts, before anything had changed. What changed was us. Later that day, we found out the camper was being totaled and a family from church offered their extra apartment for us to stay in until things worked out.

The timing of God was not lost on me. He did not resolve a thing until we asked Him to fill us with peace. He is so incredibly strategic! If He went ahead and lined everything up before we prayed, we would have gotten our peace from circumstances, rather than Him. It wasn't until we asked Him to fill us with supernatural peace regardless of our situation that He finally opened the doors. Guys I am so glad He waited! When we found a peace that wasn't attached to our surroundings, we discovered we can have peace anytime, now our peace is based on God's limitless supply not what is going on around us! We were finally free to live in peace, no matter what comes!

So yeah, I found out God made no mistake when He gave me that word for the year, because I was about to learn ALL about it! Now let's jump into this week about the shoes fitted with the Gospel of peace because there is SO much more to unpack!!!

— Amber

GOSPEL OF PEACE

Scan for session seven video

SESSION SEVEN NOTES:

DAY ONE
peace from war

It is possible to have complete peace in the middle of crazy warfare. This week is all about the gift of peace, and one of the pieces of the armor of God that brings rest in the middle of war. If the righteousness weeks were the fire, the peace week is the cool refreshing water! As we studied this attribute of the armor, we uncovered something phenomenal: Peace is actually an all-encompassing, layered word—packed full of promises that left us absolutely undone! Peace means so much more than most of us think. Without any further ado, let's start unpacking peace by reading the original Hebrew meaning of the word.

RESEARCH MORE

The Hebrew defines peace as *shalom*: completeness, soundness, welfare, peace, peace from war[10]

Y'all this is a divine piece of the armor that we have direct access to and God wants us wearing. Which definition of peace seems the most appealing to you at the moment? Why? Isn't that last definition kind of interesting? In this study, we are learning how to wear spiritual armor, but how does that fit with resting from war? We believe the war we're resting from—when it comes to peace—is not an external match with the enemy but internal. We'll explain as we go, but now that we have a better understanding of peace, let's jump in and see what the Word has to say. We're gonna start our study in the book of Isaiah, turn to chapter fifty three—a prophecy of what Jesus would do for us on the cross.

> I DELIGHT GREATLY IN THE LORD; BUT HE WAS PIERCED FOR OUR TRANSGRESSIONS, HE WAS CRUSHED FOR OUR INIQUITIES; THE _____ THAT BROUGHT US _____ WAS ON HIM, AND BY HIS WOUNDS WE ARE HEALED.
> ISAIAH 53:5 NIV

Whoah, wait, did you get that? Set upon our Savior on the cross was the punishment that brought us peace. Jesus' sacrifice has literally brought the gift of peace to us. It's kind of similar to righteousness in a way. Jesus was perfectly righteous and at the cross there was this divine exchange. Jesus wore our sin so we could wear His righteousness. Jesus also wore our punishment and turmoil and stress so we could wear His peace. What did Jesus say in John 14:27 (NIV)?

> "_____ I LEAVE WITH YOU; _____ I GIVE YOU. I DO NOT GIVE TO YOU AS THE WORLD GIVES. DO NOT LET YOUR HEARTS BE _____ AND DO NOT BE _____."

Jesus operated from a place of perfect, supernatural peace and He wants us living this way as well. The enemy is always trying to steal our peace, every day he has a plan to snatch it, and every day we have the choice to fall for His ploys or rest in the storm. But how?! How do we rest when things are raging around us? We get our peace not from earthly relationships or circumstances, we get it from an unchanging source.

In Matthew chapter six Jesus is unpacking the way to "not worry," and He gives the solution right at the end, hidden in a familiar scripture:

For the pagans run after all these things, and your heavenly Father knows that you need them. But seek first his kingdom and his righteousness, and all these things will be given to you as well. Therefore do not worry about tomorrow, for tomorrow will worry about itself. Each day has enough trouble of its own. Matthew 6:32-34 NIV

The solution to "not worrying" is preceded by seeking what two things?

1.

2.

Well, we definitely have sought His righteousness, so we're well on our way to not worrying!! But let's not forget the Kingdom of God! How do we seek that, practically?! How about we put some legs on this thing by looking at Romans chapter fourteen and fill in the blanks?!

> FOR THE _____ OF GOD IS NOT A MATTER OF EATING AND DRINKING BUT OF _____ AND _____ AND JOY IN THE HOLY SPIRIT.
> ROMANS 14:17 ESV

So right out the gate we see the Kingdom of God is not about what we eat or what drink, but it is about understanding God's righteousness—okay, check we've unpacked this. Next it lists the Kingdom of God IS what other three things?

1.

2.

3.

God's Kingdom is all about living in His righteousness, in His peace, in His joy, in His power through the Holy Spirit! How do we do this? We pray and ask our Heavenly Father to release the peace of the Kingdom of God into our hearts NOW, not when the kids act better, not when the situation works out, not when there are no issues, but now. If we only have peace when things are going good, then our peace is based on external things. But if we can operate in a supernatural peace when things are going crazy, we can have peace regardless of what is going on! This is an unshakeable peace that is available if we just seek the Kingdom of God right now! Let us get our peace from God Himself, the peace of Jesus gifted to us because of His work on the cross. If our peace comes from Him and is based on our connection to Him, it can never be taken because God cannot be taken from us.

Notice in the Romans fourteen scripture that the Kingdom IS in the Holy Spirit. We must be in relationship with the Holy Spirit in order to walk in peace. It is one of His fruits after all (Galatians 5:22). If you are struggling to have peace in your life, one of the first things we suggest is getting to know the Holy Spirit more. Read scripture on Him and ask the LORD to reveal what it looks like to have a relationship with the Holy Spirit.

Do you feel you know the Holy Spirit well?

What is one thing you can do to get closer to this person of the trinity?

When we learn to live in a place of supernatural peace we start wearing the shoes of the gospel of peace. We can find rest for our souls even among raging seas. This is resting from war internally, it's not resting from warfare though. But, having a heart at rest is warfare. You're declaring to the enemy: "You aren't stealing my peace today, buddy, its source is Jesus and His unshakeable Kingdom—a place you can't access!"

Read Philippians 4:6-7.
Write down everything that is either stealing your peace or trying to.

Then, before any of those situations have changed, pray and ask the Lord to release the supernatural peace of His Kingdom to flood your heart and mind right now.

Father, I seek your Kingdom right now, I pray the peace Jesus gave me would manifest in my heart and mind. These are the things that are causing stress in my life, I cast these cares on you, but before you fix one thing, fill me with your peace. Help me rest from all this internal warring and let me discover the secret of engaging in warfare from a place of peace.

— *Journaling* —

Journaling

DAY TWO
Prince of peace

Good news alert: We HAVE peace with God because of Jesus! The pressure is off of us to maintain peace between us and the Father . . . it is not based on us, but instead is based on the work of our Savior! Does this make anyone else want to shout hallelujah?! Peace is a part of the "good news", I mean it is actually called: The Gospel of Peace! It's a part of our promise from God! Let's begin today by looking at this truth in the Word, turn to Romans five and fill in the blanks.

> THEREFORE SINCE WE HAVE BEEN MADE _____ IN GOD'S SIGHT BY _____, WE HAVE _____ WITH GOD BECAUSE OF WHAT _____ OUR LORD HAS DONE FOR US. BECAUSE OF OUR _____, _____ HAS BROUGHT US INTO THIS PLACE OF UNDESERVING PRIVILEGE WHERE WE NOW _____, AND WE CONFIDENTLY AND JOYFULLY LOOK FORWARD TO SHARING GODS GLORY.
> ROMANS 5:1-2 NLT

We have been made right by?

(Y'all thought we were done talking about righteousness, but we just couldn't help ourselves—it's all over the Bible! Haha!)

Do we have peace with God because of what we have done or what Jesus has done?

What brings us into this place of undeserved privilege?

Y'all, this scripture is mindblowing, we don't just have access to the supernatural peace of God's Kingdom, but we also have peace with God thanks to Jesus! What a Savior!!! So often we think that our peace with God comes from our obedience or how well we've behaved, but just like with righteousness, peace is also not based on us but on Jesus' obedience!! It's all about what Jesus has done for us. The only part we have is: faith. We just have to believe it!

Let's check out how the New Covenant, the gospel, and peace all come together. Flip over to the Old Testament, because you know God has woven the gospel of peace throughout the whole Bible—He is so creative! Check out Ezekiel thirty-seven!

> I WILL MAKE A _____ OF _____ WITH THEM. IT SHALL BE AN _____ COVENANT WITH THEM. AND I WILL SET THEM IN THEIR LAND AND MULTIPLY THEM, AND WILL SET MY SANCTUARY IN THEIR MIDST FOREVERMORE. MY _____ PLACE SHALL BE WITH _____ AND I WILL BE THEIR GOD AND THEY SHALL BE MY PEOPLE. THEN THE NATIONS WILL KNOW THAT I AM THE LORD WHO SANCTIFIES ISRAEL, WHEN MY SANCTUARY IS IN THEIR MIDST FOREVERMORE.
> EZEKIEL 37:26-28 ESV

In the first verse, what does God say he will make with his people?

Incredible! Here we learn another name for the New Covenant: a covenant of peace. Part of the new deal we have with God is peace—it's part of the package!

How long will this covenant last?

This means it never ends! Now, it is important to notice when this covenant would be enacted. When He dwelled with His people. Well when did this happen? After Jesus ascended, He sent down the Holy Spirit to dwell in us! Look at these two scriptures.

> IN HIM [JESUS] YOU ALSO ARE BEING BUILT TOGETHER INTO A _____ PLACE FOR _____ BY THE SPIRIT.
> EPHESIANS 2:22 ESV

> DO YOU NOT KNOW THAT YOU ARE GOD'S _____ AND THAT GOD'S SPIRIT _____ IN YOU?
> 1 CORINTHIANS 3:16 ESV

Y'all this is for us. In the New Covenant, we are the dwelling place of the Lord. We are the temple. Again it all points to Jesus, it has nothing to do with our works, our part is faith. We need to believe we are in an everlasting covenant of peace with God because of what Jesus did!

Turn over to Isaiah nine, which is usually quoted at Christmas, but we think this needs to be pulled out all year round!

> FOR TO US A CHILD IS BORN, TO US A SON IS GIVEN, AND THE _____' WILL BE ON HIS SHOULDERS. AND HE WILL BE CALLED WONDERFUL COUNSELOR, MIGHTY GOD, EVERLASTING FATHER, PRINCE OF _____.
> ISAIAH 9:6 NIV

This passage is describing God, He is One but He is three parts: Father, Son, Holy Spirit . . . notice how each person of the trinity is described here.

When He describes Jesus—God the Son, what is He called? The Prince of?

Look at the word **government, it means rule or dominion.**[11] As we're learning today, Jesus is called the Prince of Peace because He is the ruler of our peace. He is the reason we have peace with the Father—Jesus is in charge of that, not us. It is on His shoulders, not ours. We can be weighed down with worry if we think it is up to us to maintain peace between us and God, that's not our job! That is Jesus' job! God knew we couldn't ever do that, so He sent our glorious Savior—He shoulders the weight and mediates a New Covenant between God and man! Doesn't this make you so thankful for Jesus?! Praise Him!

Walking in the shoes of the gospel of peace means so many things, but as we understand that peace is a part of the gospel, a gift God has given us through Jesus, we don't have to worry each day if we're at peace with God. We can rest knowing if our faith is in Jesus, we will never be more or less "at peace" with God than we are right now! Put those shoes on and stand confidently in Jesus' work! Truly He is the Prince of Peace!

SECRET PLACE Training

Do you ever wonder if you are truly at peace with God? Spend some time with your Heavenly Father and ask Him if you have unknowingly placed the weight of maintaining peace between you two on your shoulders, instead of Jesus? Then, ask Him to show you how to put the weight back on Jesus. Reach out to the Prince of Peace Himself and ask Him to be the ruler of your peace!

Journaling

DAY THREE
good news of wholeness

But wait, there's more! If you can believe it, peace means even more than being in a permanent place of peace with God, living free of worry, and having a heart at rest in the midst of struggles! So far we've only unpacked the Hebrew definition of peace, but the New Testament was written in Greek, so when we read peace in the New Testament it has an even deeper meaning. Look at this!

The Greek word for **peace is *eiréné*: one, peace, quietness, rest, wholeness, sense of the health of an individual**[12]

Hold up, what?! Peace isn't just about being at rest (which is awesome), it isn't just about being at peace with our Heavenly Father (which is mind-blowing—thank you, Jesus), but it also includes our WHOLENESS and HEALTH! What?!

So let's put wholeness into the Ephesians six verse about the gospel of peace: As shoes for your feet, having put on the readiness given by the gospel of wholeness. Based on Ephesians 6:15 ESV & Strong's Greek concordance.

So the gospel includes our wholeness?! God wants us whole. He does not want us operating from a broken heart, and wounded soul, a physically exhausted and sick body, or a fractured mind! He wants our heart, soul, mind, and strength completely whole and it is actually a part of the gospel. Who knew?! And, we can prove it from the words of Jesus. Fill in the blanks of this very familiar scripture!

> WHICH COMMANDMENT IS THE MOST IMPORTANT OF ALL?" JESUS ANSWERED, "THE MOST IMPORTANT IS, 'HEAR, O ISRAEL: THE LORD OUR GOD, THE LORD IS _____. AND YOU SHALL LOVE THE LORD YOUR GOD WITH ALL YOUR _____
> AND WITH ALL YOUR _____
> AND WITH ALL YOUR _____
> AND WITH ALL YOUR _____.'
> MARK 12:28B-30 ESV

What does it say that the Lord our God is?

What was the first word listed in the Greek definition of peace?

God the Father, God the Son, and God the Holy Spirit are one and they are at peace. They are completely working in tandem and united. There is not brokenness and division in God. He is whole.

Do you see how it says you shall love the Lord your God with "all" your heart, soul, mind, and strength? Well guess what that word in the Greek really means?

"All" in this verse is the Greek word: **holos- whole, complete** [13]

We are to love God with whole hearts, whole souls, whole minds, whole strength! We need every single part of us whole so we can flow in the love of God, loving Him and others in the love He has healed us with!

It is not coincidence Jesus answers this question by declaring The Lord our God is one. He is whole and He wants us to be as well, He is one and wants us to be one as well—with each other and Him!

To wear the shoes of the powerful gospel of peace means we need to get whole. Jesus died so we could be whole, not fractured, not broken but mended and put back together! Just as He healed our soul when He brought us from death to life, He wants His power to heal all of us: mind, heart, and strength included! One last scripture that we've touched on already brings this point home! Turn back to the Isaiah fifty-three description of what Jesus did for us on the cross!

But he was pierced for our transgressions; he was crushed for our iniquities; upon him was the punishment that brought us peace was on him, and by his wounds we are <u>*healed.*</u> Isaiah 53:5 ESV

Notice how the work of the cross paid the price so we could be?

Some would say "this is only spiritual healing." Does the Bible say that? Or does it simply say "healed." Healed from what? Whatever you need healing for! We want to walk in everything Jesus died for us to have, don't you agree?

Do you believe this applies to more than just spiritual healing? Why or why not? What scripture would you use to reinforce your stance?

Now, look how the following version translates peace in the same scripture:

But he was pierced for our rebellion, crushed for our sins. He was beaten so we could be <u>whole</u>. He was whipped so we could be healed.
Isaiah 53:5 NLT

It is plain as day, Jesus' work on the cross and resurrection was in part about us being able to spend eternity with the Father, but it is also so much more! Right here we see that because He took our punishment we can be healed and walk in wholeness! The gospel of peace and wholeness applies to every part of you! We're Armored Up with shoes fitting properly when we understand the gospel includes our complete wholeness!

SECRET PLACE Training

Today, spend some time with the Lord processing what we've learned. *Father, In what area of my life am I not whole? Where am I fractured? Where am I wounded?*

Write down what He shows you!

Ask Him to heal this part of you in His love and make it whole.

DAY FOUR
walking out peace

Don't say we didn't warn you—we told you peace was a very layered word. How you hanging in there? Has this been as mind-blowing to you as it was for us?! Peace seems pretty straight forward at first glance, and doesn't seem very deep, but as we begin to dig down it turns out to be a very deep well. So one of the questions we had when studying the shoes of the gospel of peace was: Why shoes? What is the significance of this being on our feet?

We ended up finding more clarity in Isaiah chapter fifty-two. Turn there and fill in the blanks.

> HOW BEAUTIFUL ON THE _____ ARE THE _____ OF THOSE WHO BRING _____, WHO PROCLAIM _____ WHO BRING GOOD TIDINGS, WHO PROCLAIM SALVATION, WHO SAY TO ZION, "YOUR GOD REIGNS!"
> ISAIAH 52:7 NLT

What is beautiful here?

Okay, interesting. Now where are the feet on top of?

Mountains can represent many things, but in the Bible the enemy especially loved establishing the mountains as his territory. Many of the altars to false gods and idols were set atop mountains. We believe God wants His people fully Armored Up to take back these mountains and turn them for the glory of God. These can represent enemy strongholds, in our lives, in the lives of others, in the church, and out in society!

But how does this connect to peace? Well notice the feet are proclaimed as beautiful —it is lovely in the eyes of God to see His people taking back the ground the enemy stole! Why feet? Because we have to walk out our peace and wholeness and we have to walk in peace and wholeness to gain the victory!

In the previous scripture, what is the person bringing and proclaiming?

1.

2.

Peace is the good news we're bringing! We've got to tell people what Jesus did for them and all He made available to them! When we walk in the shoes fitted with the good news of peace, we have put in the work to become whole, because Jesus died to bring us into full wholeness, and we are marching forward in peace. It is easy to proclaim something we have personally experienced! In order to proclaim the good news of peace and that our God reigns, we need to be people of peace! We've walked it, we've lived it!

The Lord has something beautiful hidden in a name we're all familiar with: Jerusalem. It means **city of peace or foundation of peace**!

Do you know what Hebrews 12:22 NIV says? *But you have come to Mount Zion, to the city of the living God, the heavenly Jerusalem. You have come to thousands upon thousands of angels in joyful assembly.*

The heavenly city we are a part of is a city of peace!

We are meant to be people of peace, proclaiming what Jesus has done and bringing His good news to the ends of the earth! Guess who Jesus called the "children of God" in Matthew chapter five?! Look up the scripture and complete the statement.

"BLESSED ARE THE _____, FOR THEY WILL BE CALLED CHILDREN OF GOD."
MATTHEW 5:9 NIV

As we wrap up the week of the refreshing waters of the incredible peace of God, look at one final scripture and write down the missing words to get the whole picture:

> "FOR THE MOUNTAINS MAY DEPART AND THE HILLS BE REMOVED, BUT MY STEADFAST _____ SHALL NOT DEPART FROM YOU, AND MY _____ SHALL NOT BE REMOVED," SAYS THE LORD, WHO HAS COMPASSION ON YOU. "O AFFLICTED ONE, STORM-TOSSED AND NOT COMFORTED, BEHOLD, I WILL SET YOUR STONES IN ANTIMONY, AND LAY YOUR _____ WITH SAPPHIRES. I WILL MAKE YOUR PINNACLES OF AGATE, YOUR GATES OF CARBUNCLES, AND ALL YOUR WALL OF PRECIOUS STONES. ALL YOUR CHILDREN SHALL BE TAUGHT BY THE LORD, AND GREAT SHALL BE THE _____ OF YOUR CHILDREN."
> ISAIAH 54:10-13 ESV

So much goodness. Even if every single thing in life shifts, what two things does God promise will never be removed?

1.

2.

He laid the solid foundation of Jesus with the most beautiful truths in His Word for us to stand on! When we truly receive His love and understand His covenant of peace we experience great peace! This is how we wear the shoes of the gospel of peace! We live in His peace, we war from peace, we don't let the enemy or life's circumstance steal our peace, we walk out our wholeness and healing. We believe the Word and we wage a holy war with Christ by proclaiming the peace Jesus died to give us! Just by telling people there is "peace for their souls" we snatch people out of the kingdom of darkness! We've got so much good news to share! Understanding the good news of peace and the New Covenant of peace, and walking out our peace and wholeness sets us up to take the mountains for the glory of Jesus!!!

SECRET PLACE Training

This week was a lot, we know! But we want you to take time now to really unpack everything with God. Write down what you still have questions on and what you want to learn more about. Ask the Lord to teach you about any area of peace that you are struggling to comprehend and apply.

Journaling

HELMET OF SALVATION
week eight

Take the helmet of salvation.

EPHESIANS 6:17

"I just can't seem to get free of this cycle of sin." The discouragement in the car that night was palpable, I hurt for my friend who was pouring out her heart about the anxiety she was experiencing. I pried a little further, "When you look at your situation, what do you perceive?" She went on to describe it like trying to get her head above water, but never being successful. Each time she got close this black seaweed of sin came up and wrapped around her legs, pulling her back into the depths. In this moment, something rose within me: *She needs to see herself how God does!*

After a quick silent prayer, I let the Holy Spirit guide the conversation from there. Practically, this is how that played out: The Old Testament system of having your sins removed popped in my head. Random, I know, totally out of the blue (BIG sign that the Lord gave you the idea), so I didn't question it and started talking. She was a Christian, knew the history of Israel, and was familiar with the Old Testament law and systems.

"You know in the Old Testament if a person had sin, they would bring a perfect, spotless lamb to the temple, and do you know what would happen then? The priest would inspect the lamb to make sure it was without defects. The priest ensured the sacrifice was worthy and if it passed all the requirements, it could be sacrificed on behalf of the person and the LORD would accept the offering, covering their sin. The person was then atoned for—counted righteous before God. But, I have to point out what the priest *did not* do. He did not inspect the person. The priest only looked at the sacrifice, and if the sacrifice was good, then the person would be good! Do you realize: you are as good as your sacrifice?! And who is that?"

"Jesus?" She replied, still a tad unsure.

"Yes!" I enthusiastically replied, "God is not inspecting you, He is inspecting your sacrifice! Do you believe in Jesus?! That He is the spotless Lamb of God who took away your sin?"

"Yes!" She was getting it and getting excited.

"Then you are as good as Jesus is! We are only as good as our sacrifice! God is not inspecting you! He's not looking at all . . .

your sin, He has removed it as far as the east is from the west. You are hidden in Christ forever! Do you believe this?" My tone was getting more and more enthusiastic by the second.

"Gosh, I guess I always thought He was still looking at my sin!" Light bulbs were going off.

"No! He stopped doing that at the cross! Because of your sacrifice, you are righteous, because of Jesus you have been atoned!"

"What?! It's not about my actions, but His? God is looking at Him, not me?" She was surprised, but deep down she knew it to be true.

"Girl, yes!" I emphatically replied.

"Wow. I never realized!" Breakthrough was happening.

"Well, you do now! And everytime the enemy tries to wrap his slimy seaweed or past sins around your legs and tell you: 'You aren't really free, God is still judging you!' tell Him to look at the blood! The blood of Jesus speaks forgiveness over you! His sacrifice is what God is inspecting, not you!"

"AMEN!" She shouted. That night, my friend got the gospel, and that night began her journey of being set free from an anxiety issue that had long held her in chains. Her mindset completely shifted from being sin-focused, to Savior-focused! She embraced the truth of who her sacrifice was and what He accomplished for her! She truly put on the helmet of salvation and the enemy's lies weren't going to work anymore. She knew who she was in Christ!

After this conversation, my friend was on fire like I had never seen! She began telling everyone what Jesus did for them! She led Bible studies and witnessed to women who had been to prison, were recovering from addiction, and even homeless people! The girl was as bold as a lion—which as we know is always a result of someone realizing they are righteous because of what Jesus did! Now she believed it and she told all the people! Putting on the helmet of salvation is needed to protect our minds from the enemy's schemes, but it is also imperative to us becoming a confident witness!

—Amber

HELMET OF SALVATION

Scan for session eight video

SESSION EIGHT NOTES:

DAY ONE
the renewed mind

Understanding the power of a transformed mind will unleash God's greatness in your life. When you've walked through a season of anxiety, depression, sickness, discouragement, loneliness, or defeat it's easy to feel as if you're drowning, like in this week's opening story. But when you experience the transformational power of the message of Christ and you begin to renew your mind with the Word of God, the miraculous happens. That is why this part of the armor is so special to us. It's because we learned first hand how the helmet of salvation played a critical role in winning so many battles in our life, specifically dealing with our thoughts.

The helmet of salvation is the piece of armor that protects our thought life, and we already learned last week that God paid the price so we could experience wholeness in our minds. A few of these days are a little more in-depth, but addressing our mental health is critical if we want to live in victory. Whether you currently feel like an overcomer in this area or like you're still being pulled under by the weight of your circumstance, we have an announcement: *"Salvation encompasses more than most of us realize!"* The word salvation actually means so much more than just being saved from Hell. Have you ever heard that before? Like, are you kidding me, as if that isn't good enough, there is even more?!?!?!? Yes there is, we've experienced this and continue to experience it to this day. Let's take a deeper look into what it actually means.

RESEARCH MORE

Check this out, the Greek definition for salvation is *sótéria*: **deliverance, salvation, welfare, prosperity, preservation, safety**[14]

It's such a layered word and it means so many beautiful things. Write down the six things included in the word salvation:

1.

2.

3.

4.

5.

6.

Which definition most surprises you?

Salvation speaks to so much more than just our eternity, although Heaven is obviously the home we are all longing for. In the meantime, let us not grow weary while we are still here. We must arise and take up the helmet of salvation for all it's worth and contend for our earthly deliverance with the Word of God!

But, how do we contend for our deliverance? So glad you asked. We are going after our freedom by renewing our minds with the promises of God. We start out by beginning to work out our salvation (welfare, prosperity, deliverance, preservation, and safety). As we work through today's study, keep a notebook handy and begin to write down things you need to be delivered from as they come up. We'll get to this list a little later but for now, just keep track of anything that comes to mind. Deliverance begins to take place as our belief system grows. This is why it is critical that we renew our minds. Are we speaking, thinking, and fixed on our problems or are we speaking and fixed on

our salvation that comes through faith in Jesus and His finished work? Again, we have to revive our minds and change our thoughts!

> DO NOT BE _____
> TO THE PATTERN OF THIS WORLD,
> BUT BE _____ BY THE
> _____ OF YOUR MIND.
> THEN YOU WILL BE ABLE TO
> _____ AND _____
> WHAT GOD'S WILL IS-HIS
> GOOD, _____ AND
> _____WILL.
> ROMANS 12:2 NIV

What transforms us?

One thing is for sure, without a renewed mind, we will be conformed to the patterns of this world. What does this look like practically? How do we actually renew our mind? It's pretty simple, check out the strategies in the scriptures listed next. We do this by putting second Corinthians 10:4-5 into action. Look it up and fill in the missing words.

> FOR THE _____ OF OUR _____ ARE NOT CARNAL BUT MIGHTY IN GOD FOR PULLING DOWN _____, CASTING DOWN _____ AND EVERY HIGH THING THAT EXALTS ITSELF AGAINST THE _____ OF GOD, BRINGING EVERY THOUGHT INTO CAPTIVITY TO THE _____ OF CHRIST.
> 2 CORINTHIANS 10:4-5 NKJV

What are we instructed to bring our thoughts in captivity to (which means capture the thoughts and hold it up against)?

Whose obedience?

We learned already that it was because Christ was obedient, we have the blessings of righteousness, holiness, peace, etc . . . .one way we need to renew our minds is in the truth of what Christ's obedience did for us. For instance when a thought comes in such as: I just disobeyed, I am unworthy in God's sight. I feel ashamed to even go to talk to Him. It is in this moment that we must hold this thought up to the work of Jesus. Did your obedience make a way for you to talk to your Heavenly Father in the first place, or was it Jesus' obedience? It's always been because of Jesus! After grabbing those thoughts and viewing them in light of the gospel, remember who you are in Christ! Run right to the throne of your Father who loves you, apologize, ask Him to clean you of shame, and then thank Jesus for His sacrifice that already removed this sin from your account! Doesn't it make you just want to praise your Savior?!

This verse gives us insight on how to pull down strongholds, even in our minds, by holding our thoughts up to what Jesus did! The key is to consistently grab the thoughts that do not align with the truth of the gospel and the Bible and do something about it! We take a hold of the incorrect thinking and replace it with the Word. The Bible also says we must purposely think on the right things. Look at this scripture and complete the missing words.

> FINALLY, BROTHERS AND SISTERS, WHATEVER IS _____, WHATEVER IS NOBLE, WHATEVER IS _____, WHATEVER IS PURE, WHATEVER IS _____, WHATEVER IS ADMIRABLE—IF ANYTHING IS _____ OR _____—THINK ABOUT SUCH THINGS.
> PHILIPPIANS 4:8 NIV

We love this list because not only is 'true' mentioned, but so is 'pure', 'good', and 'admirable'. Highlighting the fact that just because something is true, does not mean it is beneficial for you to think about. (For example: the news.)

We've heard it said that our thoughts are like a well traveled path. Imagine a flourishing field with one well-beaten path. If you were going to take a walk though that field, clearly you would walk on the well-beaten path, right? This is exactly what our brains do, we're going to automatically think the way we always have, unless we intentionally forge a new path.

Sometimes, we must retrain our brains and create new pathways. It's not comfortable and it takes constant effort (contending), because our brains will automatically want to go down the path it knows well. Over time, the less we travel the old and the more we trek the new, the more beaten the new path will become until the new is the norm.

We must condition our brains to take God's Word seriously. We are simply putting two verses, second Corinthians 10:4-5 and Phillipians 4:8 into action. Taking every thought captive and thinking on what is pure and right, noble . . . trustworthy, and praiseworthy. This is a divine strategy. The scriptures teach us the exact tactics we can use to defeat the enemy. It doesn't get any better than this! We have no excuse. It's been laid out plain as day for all to see.

We have to take control over our thinking and change our thought patterns. The helmet of salvation is all about our belief. In order to protect our mind, we start by taking inventory of our thoughts, then we find out what the Bible says over each one! As we declare by faith God's truth, it renews our minds and we begin to experience deliverance!

SECRET PLACE Training

Go back and review any of the things that you may have written down in your notebook throughout today's study. Are there any situations, thought patterns, or strongholds you need deliverance from?

If so, begin daily to rewire those thought patterns, with the truth from God's Word. Ask your Heavenly Father to show you some of His promises you can begin to declare over your situations. Remember it's our job to take our thoughts captive and make them obedient to Christ. That simply means don't allow things to have space in your head and heart unless they are God's truth. Pillipians 4:8 is a great scripture to examine what should stay and what should go.

Incorrect thought   *God's thought*

DAY TWO
becoming like Jesus

If we want to become physically fit, we have to do what physically fit people do. We can't just watch them (wouldn't that be nice?), believe in them, or admire them. None of that will get us closer to being like them. What we have to do is emulate them, in every way possible. We have to eat like them, sleep like them, and incorporate similar disciplines and mindsets.

Working out our salvation is no different. It's the process of becoming like Christ. Check out Romans thirteen, and let's see how it applies—fill in the blanks.

> THIS IS ALL THE MORE URGENT, FOR YOU KNOW HOW LATE IT IS; _____ IS RUNNING OUT. WAKE UP, FOR OUR _____ IS NEARER NOW THAN WHEN WE FIRST BELIEVED. THE NIGHT IS ALMOST GONE; THE DAY OF SALVATION WILL SOON BE HERE. SO REMOVE YOUR _____ _____ LIKE DIRTY CLOTHES, AND PUT ON THE _____ _____ OF RIGHT LIVING. BECAUSE WE BELONG TO THE DAY, WE MUST LIVE DECENT LIVES FOR ALL TO SEE. DON'T . . .

> PARTICIPATE IN THE DARKNESS OF WILD PARTIES AND DRUNKENNESS, OR IN SEXUAL PROMISCUITY AND IMMORAL LIVING, OR IN QUARRELING AND JEALOUSY. INSTEAD _____ _____ WITH THE PRESENCE OF THE LORD JESUS CHRIST. AND DON'T LET YOURSELF THINK ABOUT WAYS TO INDULGE YOUR EVIL DESIRES.
> ROMANS 13:11-14 NLT

Wearing the shining armor leads to?

What are we to clothe ourselves with?

This study is all about learning to live in the armor of light, clothed in Jesus. The more we look at Christ, unpack and apply the Word in our lives the more we act like Him. Jesus came to save you from an eternity in Hell and give you an eternity with Him, but He also came to save you from the here and now. Today, we're gonna learn how this is possible through the process of becoming more like Christ.

Armor Up

This doesn't mean that we won't walk through storms and tough seasons, but it does mean that Jesus can and will deliver us through them all. And in the process of trusting in Him we miraculously begin to emulate Him, especially through the trials.

> CONSIDER IT A _____ _____, MY BROTHERS AND SISTERS, WHENEVER YOU EXPERIENCE _____ _____ BECAUSE YOU KNOW THAT THE TESTING OF YOUR FAITH _____ ENDURANCE. AND LET ENDURANCE HAVE ITS FULL EFFECT, SO THAT YOU MAY BE MATURE AND COMPLETE, LACKING NOTHING. JAMES 1:2-4 CSB

We are supposed to consider trials what?

When our faith is tested, what happens?

We don't know about you, but mature and complete, lacking nothing sounds pretty much like Jesus. Are we right? Let's look at a real life example of this. Throughout His time on earth, Jesus was constantly delivering His disciples, just like He continues to deliver us.

Remember the story of Jesus calming the storm? *Then he got into the boat and his disciples followed him. Suddenly a furious storm came up on the lake, so that the waves swept over the boat. But Jesus was sleeping. The disciples went and woke him, saying, "Lord, save us! We're going to drown!" He replied, "You of little faith, why are you so afraid?" Then he got up and rebuked the winds and the waves, and it was completely calm. The men were amazed and asked, "What kind of man is this? Even the winds and the waves obey him!"* Mathew 8:23-27 NIV

You see, when Jesus quiets the storm, the disciples' fear and anxiety were immediately replaced with awe and wonder. This is how deliverance begins to happen. Again, it's based on our belief system. Now the disciples may not have had the faith to take authority over the storms, yet. But they did have faith in the One who could and that's who they called on. They called on the name of Jesus and He stopped the winds and the waves—in that instant faith was built. You see, although the disciples at this time didn't need to armor up because the One whose armor we wear was still with them and they didn't yet have an outpouring of the Holy Spirit, they would at one point have to learn to utilize the armor of Christ once He had risen.

This was their practice round. This is why Jesus responds to them, "You of little faith, why are you so afraid?" He knew they would have to build their faith and put it into action just as we do today. He was teaching them to put on the helmet of salvation. Understanding that through Christ, and our faith in Him, we would be able to grow in our belief of Him and His Word and ultimately become more and more like Christ in doing so.

> THEREFORE, IF _____ IS IN CHRIST, HE IS A _____ _____. THE OLD HAS _____ AWAY; BEHOLD, THE NEW HAS COME.
> 2 CORINTHIANS 5:17 ESV

In Christ we are?   The old has?

Think of the flourishing field that we talked about earlier this week. It's a great analogy for this scripture. We have put to death the old self and walk in the new creation that we are.

Instead of allowing the trials we go through to defeat, distract, and discourage us, let's apply what we learned in the scriptures above and use these tough seasons to our advantage. James reminds us: These struggles are used to refine us and make us more like Christ. Instead of putting our faith in ourselves or others during the difficulties, let's put it in Jesus. By trusting Him, we continue to grow in our faith and belief, and secure the helmet of salvation firm on our heads. As we close, complete this verse.

> BUT SINCE WE BELONG TO THE DAY, LET US BE SOBER, PUTTING ON FAITH AND LOVE AS A BREASTPLATE, AND THE _____ ____ _____ AS A HELMET.
> 1 THESSALONIANS 5:8 NIV

SECRET PLACE Training

So often the enemy will do his best to distract you from keeping the faith and try to get you to focus on fear. Just like any wise soldier, we have to understand the strategy of our enemy. Our problems will never get better when we focus on them, actually they will only grow worse. It's true, the neural connections in our brain grow stronger the more we think about something. This applies whether we focus on the good or the bad. The choice is ours.

Spend some time with the Lord today asking him to point out the areas in your life you focus the most on?

Are the majority of these thoughts life-giving or filled with fear and worry?

Spend some time looking up the promises of God that counter any fear-filled belief systems. Protect your thoughts by studying them and declaring them over your situations.

DAY THREE
contending for whats ours

This whole study is like a giant alarm blaring the loudest beep, beep, beep; calling us to get up, wake up, arise!!!! But particularly the helmet of salvation is a call not only to stand up but to do something. It's a call to action. It's a call to go after and take all that Jesus provided for us in His life, death, and resurrection. Just like the Isrealites had to go in and take the Promised Land, we too have to take, go after, and contend for our deliverance. How do you do this? By battling for the ground the enemy stole using the written Word of God, the sword of the Spirit—speaking and declaring scriptures in faith over your situation. Basically, you need to believe and speak. With that being said, let's dive into how to do just that.

Throughout the week we have unpacked how the helmet of salvation is understanding that while Jesus has saved us from Hell, we also have the ability through Christ to contend for our deliverance in the here and now. Salvation is simply Jesus delivering us, in whatever way we need. How beautiful is that?

Let's check out a few more scriptures and gain even more of an understanding on what it means to put on the helmet of salvation.

> FOR I AM NOT ASHAMED OF THE _____, BECAUSE IT IS THE _____ OF GOD THAT BRINGS _____ TO EVERYONE WHO _____: FIRST TO THE JEW, THEN TO THE GENTILE. FOR IN THE GOSPEL THE _____ IS REVEALED—A RIGHTEOUSNESS THAT IS BY FAITH FROM FIRST TO LAST, JUST AS IT IS WRITTEN: "THE RIGHTEOUS WILL LIVE BY FAITH."
> ROMANS 1:16-17 NIV

> SO THE GOSPEL, IS THE _____ THAT BRINGS _____?
>
> THE NEXT SENTENCE SAYS THE GOSPEL REVEALS: _____.

Well what do we have here? Righteousness again! Here it is . . .

coming back up in the helmet of salvation, because it is connected! Do you see how understanding righteousness releases the power of God to deliver people? We're not ashamed to say so, just like Paul. When we understood we were right with God because of Jesus, something exploded in us, and it catapulted the transformational process! Just understanding what Jesus did for us began changing us from the inside out! This is the power of God unto salvation!

Salvation is all about what your faith is in. Is your faith in yourself or in the work of Jesus at the cross and resurrection?

The enemy wants to trick you to believe that you are not in Christ. So much of this comes back to our identity. He wants us to "believe" that we are not clothed in Christ, that we are not righteous. If the enemy can do this and keep us focused on ourself and our flesh nature, then he can successfully deflect us from seeing and believing ourselves as you truly are, righteous by faith in Christ. When we put on the helmet of salvation we are allowing God to protect our mindset and our beliefs. It's resting in what Jesus did and believing in what's available to us because of that. Turn over to first John five and fill in the missing words.

> I HAVE WRITTEN THIS TO _____ WHO _____ IN THE NAME OF THE SON OF GOD, SO THAT YOU _____ _____ YOU HAVE ETERNAL LIFE.
> 1 JOHN 5:13 NLT

Did you catch that . . . it's for those who "believe" in the Son of God. It's John 3:16 all over again (whoever "believes" in Jesus will have eternal life).

This is not about believing in yourself or your work or whether you're good enough. It's all about what Jesus did. It's a simple mindset shift. Eyes off us, and on Jesus. Helmet of salvation in place.

Consider belief to be like a hammer. A hammer's job is to pound things in or pull things out. If the handle falls off a hammer, it can't be used effectively. It cannot easily pound nails into wood, and if the handle is missing you have no leverage to take nails out. With a damaged hammer both power and leverage are lost. It's no different in your faith. If the enemy can break our belief in what Jesus has done in us, through us, and for us, we lose both power and leverage. God has special power, gifts, and promises available for those who believe. Don't let the enemy break yours.

Look at this scripture declaring your salvation through faith in Jesus. Again, saved by belief! It's over and over throughout the scriptures. I mean come on . . . this is so exciting!

> IF YOU OPENLY _____ THAT JESUS IS LORD AND _____ IN YOUR HEART THAT JESUS IS LORD YOU WILL BE SAVED. FOR IT IS BY BELIEVING IN YOUR HEART THAT YOU ARE _____ _____. AND IT IS BY YOUR _____ THAT YOU ARE SAVED.
> ROMANS 10:9-10 NLT

Did you catch that? It's by your belief in what Jesus did and your confessions. Just to clarify, confession is not talking about saying everything you've done wrong. It's your verbal confession of your faith. Declaring with your mouth that your belief is in Jesus your LORD.

Are you wearing the helmet of Salvation and confessing and declaring the Word of God? Or are you leaving your mind open to the enemy and declaring and confessing every fear, worry, doubt that runs through your mind. We would encourage you to put on the helmet of salvation and take every ounce of deliverance that Jesus has made available to you.

SECRET PLACE Training

Now that you have a better understanding on how critical your belief system is in connection with the helmet of salvation, take some time today and ask the Lord if there are any fractures in your faith. Write down what He reveals and ask the Lord to mend and put back together any areas of brokenness.

Sometimes there are broken places in our hearts and minds that only the Lord can heal. If there is something deeply wounded in you, we beg you to take it to the Father and lay it at his feet. He is the restorer of all things. The enemy will try to use that hurt and brokenness to create a wedge between you and God. But he's a liar, he's a thief, and he's come to kill and destroy you. Jesus is your Redeemer, your Savior, the Restorer of all things. Let Him mend your wounds no matter how deep they may be. He loves you and wants to make you whole.

We want to take a quick moment and address church hurt here. If you've ever experienced church hurt in any way we encourage you to remember that our faith is in Jesus, NOT man. Men will fail us a thousand times over, but Jesus never will. He is faithful. If you've ever experienced pain in this way and feel that it has created a fracture in your faith, let the Lord mend that today.

He heals the brokenhearted and binds up their wounds. Psalm 147:3 ESV

Jesus loves you, and He wants nothing more than to restore you.

DAY FOUR
boldness before the throne

A mental war often takes place in the mind of the believer. Let's get real here for just a few moments. Thoughts like, "Am I really saved?" and, "How can I be certain?" can plague even the strongest of Christians at times. For years, both of us asked ourselves these same questions. Ever wonder, Did God really remove my sin? Well, let's see what the Bible says, fill in the missing words!

> AS FAR AS THE _____ IS FROM THE _____, SO FAR DOES HE _____ OUR TRANSGRESSIONS FROM US.
> PSALMS 103:12 ESV

Are our sins still on our account or did God cast them away, according to the Bible?

If the enemy can trip believers up, making us question our salvation, he's got way too much leverage in our life and we are not living in freedom. We know, because that used to be us! We weren't wearing our helmet of salvation because our minds were questioning if we were even saved!

Similar to this week's opening story of our friend who got free of anxiety by realizing her true identity in Christ, we too had to really understand what had been done for us and then, get this . . . accept it. Dianne had accepted Jesus as her Savior, but for a long time, she didn't think she deserved or could actually receive freedom from the web of sin surrounding her. She struggled with her worth. She didn't think Jesus' sacrifice was really sufficient. Not that she didn't think Jesus could remove her sin, it was a question of whether He would . . . for her. Can anyone relate?

Here's the reality, if the enemy can keep us here, lacking confidence, wondering about our worth, and second guessing our identity, then we stay bound—stuck in a web of lies: Questioning our salvation. We say, enough! Let's help each other escape the sticky trap of defeat and courageously step into warrior mode. Together let's learn how to walk in the fullness of our salvation!

If you are wondering if you are really saved, simply ask yourself: *Who is my faith in? Do I believe in Jesus as my Savior and sacrifice before God? Or do I believe in myself and what I have done to get me into heaven?* To help, read this verse as a reminder, and commit it to memory if you need to!

Yet we know that a person is made right with God by faith in Jesus Christ, not by obeying the law. And we have believed in Christ Jesus, so that we might be made right with God because of our faith in Christ, not because we have obeyed the law. For no one will ever be made right with God by obeying the law. Galatians 2:16 NLT

If your trust is in Jesus, you are saved, you are right with God! Helmet on! And when the thought resurfaces: *Am I saved?* You can confidently reply, "YEP, because I trust in Jesus." Pull up the stronghold and cast it out! Now let's get even more strategic by looking at a few ways we can continually guard our thoughts!

We have to protect our minds from the lies of the enemy. You truly are as good as your sacrifice. And if we believe that Jesus was the spotless lamb who gave His life for our sin, our freedom, our redemption, then how dare we let the enemy tell us otherwise. The enemy wants us anxious and fear-filled, questioning every promise of God. But God wants you to live in peace, confidently stepping into all He has for you!

Simply put, we need to detox our brain from all of the lies of the enemy and begin filling it with the life-giving diet of truth. Circle the correct statement below each verse.

> YOU KEEP HIM IN _____ _____ WHOSE MIND IS STAYED ON YOU, BECAUSE HE TRUSTS YOU.
> ISAIAH 26:3 ESV

We have peace when our minds are focussed on ourselves/the LORD.

> FOR TO SET THE _____ ON THE FLESH IS _____, BUT TO SET THE _____ ON THE _____ IS LIFE AND PEACE.
> ROMANS 8:6 ESV

We experience abundant life when we focus on the flesh/the Spirit.

> DO NOT BE ANXIOUS ABOUT _____, BUT IN EVERY SITUATION, BY _____ AND _____, WITH THANKSGIVING, PRESENT YOUR REQUESTS TO GOD. AND THE _____ OF GOD, WHICH TRANSCENDS ALL UNDERSTANDING, WILL GUARD YOUR HEARTS AND YOUR _____ IN CHRIST JESUS.
> PHILIPPIANS 4:6-7 NIV

We should be anxious about some things/nothing.

If this is an instruction, it must be possible . . . but only with God's help! As we begin to understand salvation, we confidently start walking in truth and it's then that we can go boldly before God in prayer. It's okay to bring your situation before the LORD, but we must cast the cares on Him and trust He will bring us His peace to guard our minds from worry. When you experience the peace of God, the enemy can no longer torment you.

Y'all, we have the mind of Christ! Wait, before you move on, let that sink in. We have been given the ability to think like Jesus!!!!

> FOR, "WHO CAN KNOW THE LORD'S _____? WHO KNOWS ENOUGH TO TEACH HIM?" BUT WE _____ THESE THINGS, FOR WE HAVE THE _____ OF _____.
> 1 CORINTHIANS 2:16 NLT

We have the mind of Christ/of a sinner.

> IT'S NOT NO LONGER _____ WHO LIVE, BUT _____ WHO LIVES IN US, THE LIFE I NOW LIVE IN THE FLESH I LIVE _____ _____ IN THE SON OF GOD WHO LOVED ME AND GAVE HIMSELF FOR ME.
> GALATIANS 2:20 ESV

This life I live, I live by faith in myself/the Son of God who loved me.

When we begin to . . .

- train our brains to take every thought captive and view it through the obedience of Christ
- think on the virtues listed in Philippians 4:8
- trust in the Word of God and allow Him to transform us into His likeness through the trials of this life
- abide in the scriptures and protect our minds from the schemes of the enemy

. . . we will begin to rest in his peace, giving us peace of mind. This is how we walk out wholeness in our mental health, this is the process by which we renew our minds. Let's finish securing the helmet of salvation by spending some time in the secret place processing all we've learned.

What does the helmet of salvation mean to you? What does it have to do with deliverance?

Do you struggle with anxiety, fear, depression, loneliness, sadness, or anything opposite of peace? If so, ask the LORD to reveal any lies keeping you captive. Today break that agreement in the name of Jesus and continue to declare God's Word over your situation.

Why is the enemy after your mind and what can you do to protect it?

Journaling

SWORD OF THE SPIRIT
week nine

Take the sword of the Spirit which is the word of God.

EPHESIANS 6:17

I was too embarrassed to let anyone know the reality of our situation. We were in way over our heads. The student loans, medical bills, enormous IRS payment, and every other debt we had managed to accumulate was swallowing us whole. Literally, we felt lost in a sea of never-ending bills, and our boat was about to capsize. We felt hopeless, overwhelmed, and didn't think anyone could truly relate.

I cannot tell you what claiming God's promises over our lives during this season did for us. Let me just say, this is not magic, positive affirmation, genie-in-a-bottle stuff. It's simply God's truth. I wrote out verses I found in God's Word regarding finances and posted them everywhere in my home. Little did I know that incorporating this little habit of declaring scripture out loud, was about to change the trajectory of our lives forever. Something very powerful takes place when you begin to speak God's Word over your circumstances. As you begin to declare scripture, it takes root in your head and heart and you begin to believe it, like really, truly believe it for you. It doesn't take long before you notice a shift taking place in you and or your situation. There is literally no way to . . .

describe what happened next, except a miracle—an absolutely, amazing miracle! I'm not promising that your debt will miraculously disappear, but I am suggesting that God will work in mysterious ways. I believe wholeheartedly that God blesses those who are generous and those who make it a point to give their first fruits to Him—we see this throughout the Bible. For many years in our life, tithing was very sacrificial. It was hard. We had to make the choice weekly between tithing or buying groceries. As hard as it was, we always put tithing first. Here are two things if you are at this point in life: One, you are not alone! I have been there and can relate. Two, trust God and give what you can to Him. Ask Him to lead and guide you in this area. In the New Testament we're not told how much to give to the LORD, but we are unveiled the spiritual principle of sowing and reaping (Galatians 6:7-9, Luke 6:38). We cannot reap from the Kingdom of God if we do not sow into the Kingdom of God.

Remember that tithing or giving is more of a heart issue than a money issue. For us, we decided that we would be faithful in our tithing just like we were faithful in our marriage. Side note, we never went hungry.

As a matter of fact, it brings me to tears as I recall during this season: Four different times groceries were delivered to our door, simply because God put it on someone's heart to do so. He is so faithful.

So what did we do to help change our financial situation? Our family decided to give to God out of our first fruits, no matter what our bank account status was. We chose to believe God wanted us to experience His greatness, even in the area of finances. We stood on the promises in the Word of God (which I was constantly reminded of because they were on notecards plastered all over our house).

One day years later I said to my husband, "Do you remember the day I listed everything I was going to speak God's promises over? Remember how overwhelmed we were with life circumstances? How with our income and situation, there seemed no realistic way out? Do you know that I just looked at that list a few days ago, and every single thing listed is completely wiped out?" In five years, everything was gone! What would have taken us more than a lifetime to eliminate by our own standards, God had eliminated. In our finances, there's no way to explain where we are at, except the faithfulness of God!

I put my faith, my hope, and my trust in Him and in His Word. I didn't deserve it, but He challenged me to believe His promises in . . . every one of these areas. He taught me to retrain my brain using His truth and dollar store notecards ('cuz that is all I could afford)! I spoke out what the Bible said about finances, blessing, and His provision way before I saw it come to fruition! But little by little, the spoken Word of God did not come back void!

We worked hard; don't get me wrong. We spoke the Word and got to work! We sacrificed things to pay stuff off; we took action in the areas that He said to take action in. We not only believed, but we did. We did whatever God told us to do. He multiplied our efforts, and we discovered that there is supernatural favor on those who believe "with God all things are possible".

Some of you may be thinking, that's crazy! You can't just expect great things to happen because you post notecards with Bible verses on them in your home and read them aloud every day. All I have to say is if you think it won't happen, you're exactly right. If you speak that, believe that, then I promise you, you will experience just that. You'll get no change.

You must have hope. You must have faith in what God says. You can read the healing stories in the Bible all day long, but if you don't believe they really happened and God is the same yesterday, today, and forever, then my guess is you won't grasp His greatness in that area. But, once you understand God's character, you'll reap the rewards in every area of your life in even greater measure. Things aren't always good, but He will work them together for our good if we let Him.

When I began speaking out the scriptures on the promises of God, I picked up the sword of the Spirit and used it! This weapon is mighty indeed! The Word of God began to reform our reality, right before our eyes! I partnered with God's truths and shifted our situation and so can you!

—Dianne

SWORD OF THE SPIRIT

Scan for session nine video

SESSION NINE NOTES:

DAY ONE
the power of words

The sword of the Spirit is the only weapon the Lord provides for us in the armor of God. Everything else is for defense. We're super passionate about this topic, because both of us have received and experienced so much freedom from using the sword of the Spirit. This is the only offensive piece God has armed us with as it's the only weapon we need. Remember, our battle is not against flesh and blood but against the spiritual forces of darkness, so we need to wield a spiritual weapon to be effective. Think about the time that Jesus was in the desert for forty days, when the enemy came to tempt Him, what did He do? Well, flip over to Luke four and read through the scriptures. Pay attention to how Jesus responds to the enemy's attack and temptation by filling in His responses.

> THEN JESUS WAS LED UP BY THE SPIRIT INTO THE WILDERNESS TO BE TEMPTED BY THE DEVIL. AND AFTER FASTING FORTY DAYS AND FORTY NIGHTS, HE WAS HUNGRY. AND THE TEMPTER CAME AND SAID TO HIM, "_____ _____ _____ THE . . .

> SON OF GOD, COMMAND THESE STONES TO BECOME LOAVES OF BREAD." BUT HE ANSWERED, "____ ____ _____, "'MAN SHALL NOT LIVE BY BREAD ALONE, BUT BY EVERY WORD THAT COMES FROM THE MOUTH OF GOD.'" THEN THE DEVIL TOOK HIM TO THE HOLY CITY AND SET HIM ON THE PINNACLE OF THE TEMPLE AND SAID TO HIM, "_____ _____ THE SON OF GOD, THROW YOURSELF DOWN, FOR IT IS WRITTEN, "'HE WILL COMMAND HIS ANGELS CONCERNING YOU,' AND "'ON THEIR HANDS THEY WILL BEAR YOU UP, LEST YOU STRIKE YOUR FOOT AGAINST A STONE.'" JESUS SAID TO HIM, "AGAIN ____ ____ _____, 'YOU SHALL NOT PUT THE LORD YOUR GOD TO THE TEST.'" AGAIN, THE DEVIL TOOK HIM TO A VERY HIGH MOUNTAIN AND SHOWED HIM ALL THE KINGDOMS OF THE WORLD AND THEIR GLORY. AND HE SAID TO HIM, "ALL THESE I WILL GIVE YOU, IF YOU WILL FALL DOWN AND WORSHIP ME." THEN JESUS SAID TO HIM, "BE GONE, SATAN! FOR _____ _____, "'YOU SHALL WORSHIP THE LORD . . .

> YOUR GOD AND HIM ONLY SHALL YOU SERVE.'" THEN THE DEVIL _____ HIM, AND BEHOLD, ANGELS CAME AND WERE MINISTERING TO HIM.
> MATTHEW 4:1-11 ESV

When the enemy attacked and tempted Jesus, how did Jesus always respond?

Right, He replied with "it is written" and quoted scripture. After three times of being tempted, Jesus answered with three Bible verses, and what happened?

We can't miss this. The devil has to leave when scripture is consistently spoken! The Word is more than he can take. Often, when we face a spiritual attack, we don't always know where to start. But we don't need to overcomplicate spiritual warfare, if we want to experience the results Jesus did, we need to do exactly what He did! Speak the Word of God!

First, Jesus knew who He was (the Son of God). Second, He simply declared the Word of God and it stopped the enemy in his tracks. The truth is, the enemy can not stand against a believer who knows their identity and authority in Christ, and has the scriptures on their lips, it's his weakness.

Let's unpack this story a little more by looking at the strategy of the enemy so we know how to use our weapon. The devil and his demons are always lying, taking things out of context, twisting the truth, manipulating, and deceiving every situation, scenario, and issue we encounter and he will always play on our weakness. Always! Now Jesus didn't have a weakness but notice how the enemy still attacked Jesus' identity, power, authority, Sonship, and Lordship. But what did Jesus do in every one of these attacks, accusations, and temptations? He wasn't phased, didn't feel the need to prove He was the Son of God (He knew it), and proceeded to confidently declare the truth of God's Word (He said it).

Did you notice that the enemy knows the Bible and that he will blatantly misuse scripture in an attempt to manipulate us and our situation? This reminds us how imperative it is that we study the Bible on our own. We must know it. One of the biggest takeaways from this scripture is: The Word of God does not become a weapon until we speak it. The enemy can not read your mind, so while memorizing the Word of God is critical, (as it builds your faith, and brings wisdom and understanding), in order for it to take the enemy out you must speak it, you must put breath into it.

By now you probably have picked up on the fact that we love looking up the original context of scripture. We hope it helps bring a deeper level of understanding. Well, we don't want to let ya down so we've done it for you again!

If you look up the Greek word for Spirit in Ephesians 6:17 it is *pneuma*: wind, breath, spirit [15]

RESEARCH MORE

So, take a look at how this definition provides more clarity about the weapon in the armor of God: The "sword of the Spirit" could be viewed as the "sword of breath" . . . isn't that enlightening? It becomes the weapon of our breath when we speak the Word of God, it's His Holy Spirit in us partnering with our words. Declaring the holy scriptures outloud to the enemy takes him out! This is the weapon God has given us to wield and it works, if we use it.

This brings up a very powerful question. What are you speaking? The reason this is important is because your answer to this question will often determine the outcome of your situation. Let's look at what the Word says.

> _____ AND _____ ARE IN THE POWER OF THE _____ AND THOSE WHO LOVE IT EAT ITS FRUITS.
> PROVERBS 18:21 ESV

This scripture is incredible. Whether we speak good or bad, negative or positive, death or life, the words coming out of our mouth hold power. Now imagine if there is power in our everyday ordinary words, how much more power do the words of God hold? I mean come on . . . we need to be taking advantage of this weapon every chance we get! Notice there is no gray area here. There is no "on the fence"—what we say either gives life or it brings forth death. What we speak carries more power than most realize. Actually, we would argue that the spoken Word of God is the most underutilized weapon in the life of most believers.

> FOR THE WORD OF GOD IS _____ AND _____ SHARPER THAN ANY TWO-EDGED SWORD, PIERCING TO THE DIVISION OF SOUL AND OF SPIRIT, OF JOINTS AND OF MARROW, AND DISCERNING THE _____ AND _____ OF THE HEART.
> HEBREW 4:12 ESV

How does this verse describe God's Word?

1.

2.

3.

4.

5.

It's absolutely fascinating to wrap our minds around the fact that the Bible is alive and active. Let that resonate for just a moment. The words of God are actually alive. They are actively doing something. They are at work when the words are being read, but they are put into further action when spoken! When we use our breath to speak the Word of God it sends them out on a mission. We are literally calling forth the promises of God!

What would happen if we started declaring what the Word of God says is available to us? Would our life begin looking a little different? What would shift if we guarded what we said and only declared things that give life? What would it look like to refuse to come into agreement with anything that does not align with the scriptures? As we dust off our—perhaps underused—weapon, and boldly declare the truth of God's Word over the attacks of the enemy, our circumstances and outcomes will begin to change! When the body of Christ as whole does this, we're not just protected from attack, we're fighting back! We would be slaying demons left and right, and walking in the freedom, blessings, protection, and favor of God every minute of every day! We're not saying the fight will end, or attacks will stop, they won't. We will experience troubles in this world. What we are saying is we now know what to do in the battle! Just like the example that Jesus gave us while being tempted in the desert, when the scriptures are spoken the enemy is powerless. He cannot stand up against the Word of God, so let's pick up our swords and start swinging!

SECRET PLACE Training

Take inventory of your thoughts and evaluate where you think the enemy tempts you most.

How can you incorporate the example of Jesus when you feel attacked and bombarded by the enemy?

DAY TWO
winning the battle

Maybe you're wondering how there is actual power in our words. Let's go all the way back to Genesis and revisit how God created the world. Do you remember? God literally spoke the world into existence, He created it with His words. Think about this, nothing appeared until God first called it forth. Now, remember when He created Adam? What did He say?

> THEN GOD SAID, "LET US MAKE MANKIND IN OUR _____, IN OUR _____, SO THAT THEY MAY RULE OVER THE FISH IN THE SEA AND THE BIRDS IN THE SKY, OVER THE LIVESTOCK AND ALL THE WILD ANIMALS, AND OVER ALL THE CREATURES THAT MOVE ALONG THE GROUND."
> GENESIS 1:26 NIV

Mankind (male and female) our made like God in two ways:

1.

2.

We were created to resemble and be like God. Therefore, we do as He did. If His words carried power to change the atmosphere, in some ways, ours do too! We are not all-powerful as God is. But, we know from studying the effects on a plant when negative words are spoken versus positive, the former shrivels while the latter thrives. Our words do hold power to curse and bless. What we speak, we create! Isn't that fascinating? Have you ever considered we are like God in this way?

So the truth is, what you think about, you speak about, and actually does come about. Amber shares a great example of this in the video from this week. When someone spoke something offensive to her she became very guarded and angry. She evaluated her livid emotions and immediately chose to speak out the Word over the anger that was rising: "The love of God in me is not easily angered" and her emotions instantly changed. This is the first time she recognized the power of the spoken Word of God—it changed her life!

Turn in your Bible to first Samuel seventeen and check out the story of David and Goliath one more time. Most people believe that David won the battle with Goliath when he pulled out his sling and struck him with a stone. However, we'd like to highlight what David did before he ever pulled a stone out of his shepherd's bag. Let's look at what David declared before the victory was his.

> "THIS DAY THE LORD _____ _____ _____ INTO MY HAND, AND I WILL _____ YOU DOWN AND CUT OFF YOUR HEAD. AND I WILL GIVE THE DEAD BODIES OF THE HOST OF THE PHILISTINES THIS DAY TO THE BIRDS OF THE AIR AND TO THE WILD BEASTS OF THE EARTH, THAT ALL THE EARTH MAY KNOW THAT THERE IS A GOD IN ISRAEL."
> 1 SAMUEL 17:46 ESV

We believe it was when David declared these truths that he won the battle. He prophesied the truth of who God was and what God was going to do through him. David proclaimed five different truths and called them all into existence—then every one came to pass. When we declare scripture we are partnering with God to experience His miraculous provision and power.

There's still more, if you can you believe it!

> "NO _____ FORGED AGAINST YOU WILL _____, AND YOU WILL _____ EVERY _____ THAT ACCUSES YOU. THIS IS THE _____ OF THE LORD, AND THIS IS THEIR VINDICATION FROM ME," DECLARES THE LORD
> ISAIAH 54:17 NIV

> WILL WEAPONS BE FORGED AGAINST US?
> THIS SCRIPTURE SAYS THEY WILL NOT PROSPER IF YOU WILL _____ EVERY TONGUE THAT ACCUSES YOU.

What does this mean? We must choose to disarm the weapon coming against us by using our words to refute the attack. We have to do something about it! Why? Because this is the inheritance of the saints of the LORD, that God has given us the privilege to have authority over the attack! He's given us His Word to counterattack, just like Jesus!

Did you get that you have to refute, you have to disprove, you have to speak against what is going against you, and this is exactly what David did?! He refuted the tongue that came against him (which essentially said he was a small, little boy with a stick) and we can too. Together, let's learn the promises of God and declare them over our situations. Remember the power of life and death are in the tongue! Pick up your very potent weapon of God, and use the sword of the Spirit to refute every attack with the truth of God's Word!

Journaling

SECRET PLACE TRAINING

The spiritual principle of our "words carry power" works—whether we speak good or bad. In the scripture we looked at today, we see the power of life and death lies within what we say—this applies to agreements—what we have verbally agreed with. Have you made an agreement with something that doesn't line up with the Word of God? (This can be in health, finances, your family, about others, etc . . .) If so, break that agreement in the name of Jesus and start declaring what God says about you and your situation. What we say shapes our lives, be careful what you speak and what you allow others to speak over you.

Pray this: *God, bring to my attention any agreements I have made that aren't in alignment with your promises. Reveal any areas I am not speaking life.*

You may want to grab a notepad and write them down. Then, one-by-one break every negative agreement that you've made in the mighty name of Jesus. This is such a powerful way to swing your sword. If we change our words we change our world!

DAY THREE
the changed name

Imagine being 100 years old and your life is about to change forever! No, we're not referring to the end of life but the exact opposite: New life! What if you found yourself having a baby, at the ripe old age of one hundred y'all???!!! One. Hundred. Years. Old. What???? Man, God sure does have a sense of humor! This actually happened, let's check out the story. Turn to Genesis chapter twelve, when God calls a man named Abram to follow Him, will pick up the story right there. Fill in the missing word to complete the verse.

> THEN THE LORD APPEARED TO ABRAM AND SAID, "TO YOUR _____ I WILL GIVE THIS LAND."
> GENESIS 12:7 ESV

Who is the LORD giving the land to?

> "ALL THE LAND THAT YOU SEE I WILL GIVE TO _____ AND YOUR _____ FOREVER. I WILL MAKE YOUR OFFSPRING LIKE THE DUST OF THE EARTH,
> SO THAT IF ANYONE COULD COUNT THE DUST, THEN YOUR OFFSPRING COULD BE COUNTED. GO, WALK THROUGH THE LENGTH AND BREADTH OF THE LAND, FOR I AM GIVING IT TO YOU."
> GENESIS 13:15-17 NIV

Here we see a continual confirmation of the promise, but notice who keeps declaring the promise. Is it God or Abram?

Lets jump ahead to where the power of the spoken word of God makes its debut. Complete the verses by filling in the missing words.

> WHEN _____ WAS NINETY-NINE YEARS OLD, THE LORD APPEARED TO HIM AND SAID, "I AM GOD ALMIGHTY; WALK BEFORE ME FAITHFULLY AND BE BLAMELESS. THEN I WILL MAKE MY COVENANT BETWEEN ME AND YOU AND WILL GREATLY INCREASE YOUR NUMBERS . . ."

> ABRAM FELL FACEDOWN, AND GOD SAID TO HIM, "AS FOR ME, THIS IS MY COVENANT WITH YOU: YOU WILL BE THE _____ OF MANY NATIONS. NO LONGER WILL YOU BE CALLED _____;
> YOUR NAME WILL BE _____, FOR I HAVE MADE YOU A FATHER OF MANY NATIONS. I WILL MAKE YOU VERY FRUITFUL; I WILL MAKE NATIONS OF YOU, AND KINGS WILL COME FROM YOU. I WILL ESTABLISH MY COVENANT AS AN EVERLASTING COVENANT BETWEEN ME AND YOU AND YOUR DESCENDANTS AFTER YOU FOR THE GENERATIONS TO COME, TO BE YOUR GOD AND THE GOD OF YOUR DESCENDANTS AFTER YOU."
> GENESIS 17:1-7 NIV

What did God change Abram's name to?

This is fascinating, because get this: Abraham in Hebrew actually means "father of nations". Why did God do this and what in the world does this have to do with the sword of the Spirit? Two reasons. First, the LORD changed Abram's identity into who he was meant to become. Second, we believe it was God's intention to give Abram no choice but to declare the promise of who God said he was with his very own breath—causing him to put the sword of the Spirit into action. Every time he introduced himself as Abraham, or someone called his name, it proclaimed "you are the father of many"! His name became a prophetic declaration of God's word! Look what happened next!

And Sarah conceived and bore Abraham a son in his old age at the time of which God had spoken to him. Genesis 21:2 ESV

After God changed His name, it took less than a year of faithfully declaring God's word over his life—after decades with no heir—for the promise to be fulfilled. Y'all, it takes nine months to have a baby and it was in that year's time that Isaac was born. You do the math, and look how fast things changed for Abraham. Look at what declaring God's truth and promises over our life will do! It doesn't always happen overnight, but as soon as we understand our new identity in Christ and pick up the sword of the Spirit, a seed is planted . . . and over time it grows and produces fruit in our life! Complete the following verses!

> "THE RAIN AND SNOW COME DOWN FROM THE HEAVENS AND STAY ON THE GROUND TO WATER THE EARTH. THEY CAUSE THE GRAIN TO _____ . . .

> PRODUCING _____ FOR THE FARMER AND BREAD FOR THE HUNGRY. IT IS THE SAME WITH MY _____ I SEND IT OUT, AND IT ALWAYS _____. IT WILL ACCOMPLISH ALL I WANT IT TO, AND IT WILL _____ EVERYWHERE I SEND IT."
> ISAIAH 55:10-11 NLT

God's spoken Word always makes an impact! Now, taking one last look at Abraham, we'll end the story here:

Abraham was a hundred years old when his son Issac was born to him. Genesis 21:5 ESV

Why do you think God waited until Abraham was a hundred before He blessed him with the promise of Issac, the son that would lead him into the ultimate promise of being a father of nations? We'd like to suggest that perhaps God wasn't waiting to fulfill His end of the promise, but maybe, just maybe Abraham hadn't fulfilled his. If you go back and read the whole story, you'll notice that Abraham even tried to take a shortcut to fulfill this promise in his own strength, but it didn't work out so well for him. As it never does when we take things into our own hands. But what if God was waiting for Abraham to pick up the sword of the Spirit and use it? What if God was waiting for Abraham to breathe life into His promise, by speaking it? Remember God's Word is alive and active, when we speak it, we send His words out on a mission. Once Abraham's name changed and his destiny was consistently being declared, the Word got to work!

The sword of the Spirit is powerful. The Bible is FULL of promises, but maybe like Abraham, we haven't seen them come to fruition, because perhaps we have not been speaking them, or maybe we needed an identity shift like Abraham, perhaps we didn't fully know who we were in Jesus? It's okay, we know now! Let's get the Word of God on our lips and begin to prophesy our destiny! This is something to get excited about, because the same power that was available to Abraham and Sarah, and Jesus, is what we have inside of us—the Holy Spirit.

> THE _____ OF GOD, WHO RAISED JESUS FROM THE DEAD, LIVES IN YOU. AND JUST AS GOD RAISED CHRIST JESUS FROM THE DEAD, HE WILL GIVE _____ TO YOUR MORTAL BODIES BY THIS SAME _____ LIVING WITHIN YOU.
> ROMANS 8:11 NLT

Armor Up

Life comes to our mortal body through who?

We use the weapon of the Spirit when we speak the Word, this is how we will experience more abundant life!

Journaling

SECRET PLACE Training

Can you think of a promise God has given you that hasn't come to pass yet?

If so, write it out and start declaring it out loud today. Repeat that promise over your life with faith and confidence just like Abraham did time and time again.

Maybe you're wondering how to tell if God spoke a promise over you. If you aren't sure, do not be discouraged, be encouraged. Ask God to reveal what He has for you, what His plan is and get into His Word to see what He says. God speaks to all of us in different ways, but He always speaks to us through His Word.

Look up John 10:27-28, Jeremiah 33:3, and Hebrews 4:12. How do these scriptures build your faith in God's voice and the Word of God?

Journaling

DAY FOUR
mountain moving faith

When we stand between the mountain and the miracle, what we say matters. Today, we're going over practical teaching which leads to miraculous outcomes. Impossible situations are about to meet miracle working power, and we are simply the conduit. Now, before we dive in please hear us out, this does not mean that because you declare something in faith it's automatically going to happen (although it could) or if it doesn't happen don't assume that you lack faith. What we are saying is to ask yourself the following: First, does what you're declaring line up with the Word of God, or is it actual scripture? Second, we have to keep in mind two very important scriptures when holding things up to the Bible.

> *"For my thoughts are not your thoughts neither are your ways my ways," declares the LORD. "As the heavens are higher than the earth, so are my ways higher than your ways and my thoughts than your thoughts."*
> Isaiah 55:8-9 NIV

God's ways and thoughts are higher than ours. With that in mind, He will never go back on His word. His "ways" also include His timing. We often don't know God's timeline, usually we're in a hurry and can get discouraged if what we are declaring doesn't happen as quick as we feel it should, or if He chooses to heal in a different way or bring the the ultimate breakthrough in Heaven. Even if a situation doesn't pan out the way we had hoped or desired, it doesn't mean that God isn't at work or that speaking His Word isn't working. Remember, His Word does not return void (Isaiah 55:11).

> *And we know that in all things God works for the good of those who love him, who have been called according to his purpose.*
> Romans 8:28 NIV

Not everything we face will be good, no matter what we speak. Trials will come, that's a no brainer. The Bible is very clear on that. Using the sword of the Spirit isn't about avoiding problems.

It's about facing and fighting them confidently armed with God's truth. This is not wishful thinking or a genie-in-a-bottle teaching. That's what the enemy wants you to walk away believing and not put any of this into practice. This is simply putting into action the power-packed Word of God and believing that all things, the good and the bad are promised to work for our good.

Jesus unveils more about this supernatural weapon available to us in Matthew, let's see what He has to say, fill in the missing words to complete the scripture.

> "TRULY I TELL YOU, IF YOU HAVE _____ AS SMALL AS A MUSTARD SEED, _____ CAN _____ TO THIS MOUNTAIN, "_____ FROM HERE TO THERE, AND IT WILL MOVE. _____ WILL BE IMPOSSIBLE FOR YOU."
> MATHEW 17:20 NIV

Does Jesus tell us to ask Him to move the mountain?

Who does He instruct to speak to the mountain (which represents obstacles)?

Most people think this scripture is all about faith and well, it is, but there is a very important part of this scripture that if not acted on, could leave you faith-filled, but likely miracle-less. We're not suggesting that God needs us in any way to do anything but we are suggesting that when Jesus gives us specific directions on how to accomplish miraculous outcomes that we pay very close attention to the details.

Focus on this little phrase: "you say". Notice Jesus doesn't say, "Ask God, beg, plead, hope, and fret." Instead Jesus is telling us to "say to this mountain". Yes, we have to speak to our mountains yet often we find ourselves asking and begging God to speak to them for us. Sometimes we ask God to move things on our behalf, but perhaps the LORD is waiting for us to command the obstacles to move in the authority He gave us, according to the promises found in the scriptures.

The gospel of Mark also records Jesus saying this, but pay attention to the last sentence! Look it up and fill in the blanks.

> SO JESUS ANSWERED AND SAID TO THEM, "HAVE FAITH IN _____. FOR ASSUREDLY, I SAY TO YOU, _____ SAYS TO THIS . . .

> MOUNTAIN, 'BE REMOVED AND BE CAST INTO THE SEA,' AND DOES NOT DOUBT IN HIS HEART, BUT _____ THAT THOSE THINGS ____ _____ WILL BE DONE, HE WILL HAVE WHATEVER _____.
>
> MARK 11:22-23 NKJV

What is our faith supposed to be in?

Next, Jesus reveals the significance of what we speak. Fill in the blank of the last statement one more time:

> HE WILL HAVE WHATEVER _____.

This is proof that what we say is important! So we speak to the mountain, backed with scriptures that apply to the situation, and God moves it! Our faith works in tandem with our words!

Look at what the book of Romans says here regarding the story of Abraham and how this fits with the words of Jesus in the verses above. Turn to Romans chapter four and fill in the blanks.

> AS IT IS WRITTEN: "I HAVE MADE YOU A FATHER OF MANY NATIONS." HE IS OUR FATHER IN THE SIGHT OF GOD, IN WHOM HE BELIEVED - THE GOD WHO GIVES _____ TO THE DEAD AND _____ _____ _____ THINGS THAT WERE NOT.
>
> ROMANS 4:17 NIV

God created the world by speaking first, then it formed. Similarly, when He switched Abram's name to Abraham He called something into existence. We know we are made in His likeness, and we believe Jesus in the book of Mark and Paul in the book of Romans are sharing the same message, "You have the ability to call forth what's not, you have the ability through My word, the Word of God to tell your mountain to move and it has to go!" He has given us the authority but in faith, we have to put it into action through our voice. The enemy wants us defeated by our mountains, situations, and obstacles that seem so big we quit before we even try to take it out. But God's plan is different, He didn't leave us powerless. Turns out we just have to use the one and only spiritual weapon He's given us and that's His Word.

We must declare with faith, not doubting.

Notice in the armor what two things are for us to hold in our hands? It's the sword of the Spirit and the shield of faith. That's because they go hand in hand. We can not effectively use the sword of the Spirit without faith in what the Bible says. It's put together so perfectly.

We have to get really good at declaring in faith the end before the beginning. The goal is to keep speaking, keep believing, and keep growing in the Word of God and in our relationship with Him. For His promises are always yes and amen.

> FOR ALL THE _____ OF GOD IN HIM ARE YES, AND IN HIM AMEN, TO THE GLORY OF GOD _____ US.
> 2 CORINTHIANS 1:20 NKJV

It does not say that our desires and our perceived outcomes are yes and amen, but God's promises—what He has actually promised in the Bible. The sword of the Spirit is put into action when we know the promises found in the Word and speak them. Our words have power and when what we say aligns with what the LORD has said, it's like double power—truly a double edged sword!

SECRET PLACE Training

Have you struggled in the past with questioning your faith because something didn't turn out as you had hoped or expected?

If so, ask God to come in and heal that place in your heart and mind. Not everything will turn out how we want, but everything will be worked for the good of those who love God (Romans 8:28) and for His glory. We have to trust that He is good and He is for us. Remember it's in the trials that we grow the most. If there is never a trial, if we never had anything to fight through, we'd never need a weapon or armor. Right?

Journaling

SHIELD OF FAITH
week ten

In all circumstances take up the shield of faith with which you can extinguish all the flaming darts of the evil one.

EPHESIANS 6:16

I've always dreamed of owning a white farmhouse. I grew up running barefoot through the steamy grass and fields of beautiful North Carolina farmland. Something about raising my kids on a farm just seems like home. Years and years ago, I felt the Lord promise "One day, you'll have one." I've held on to this promise ever since.

While working towards acquiring funds to purchase land to build our farm we ran into obstacle after obstacle. First, hardly any banks were loaning on land and second, we are self-employed and considered "too risky." In short, we were turned down multiple times. It was a very hard season. At the time, we were living in a small camper on my parents property—no, not the one that was wrecked by a tree, this was before. It has been a journey to say the least. We couldn't find a rental in our price range or a house we wanted, and now the banks were turning us down?! It felt like our promise was so far out of reach. We kept believing God could do it, but I won't lie, we were discouraged at the size of the mountain that stood before us. My prayers during this time sounded a little something like: *Lord, how can I get my farm? Make a way so I can . . . get this farm. Father, why is nothing moving?* As long as I prayed for what I wanted, nothing ever changed. But one night it hit me: Why don't I pray for what God wants? Hello! I had honestly not thought of that. One Saturday evening I got honest before the Lord. Father, I am sorry I've only been asking for what I want. What do you want for us? I want to do what you ask.

I didn't get an immediate answer but I did feel an immediate shift in me. The next day during our church service, God spoke to me during worship, and asked if I would travel for Him? To which I replied, "Yes." Then He took it a step further, "Would you give up your farm for me?" I did not answer as quickly. What? Give up the home He had promised? This cut deep. I felt like Abraham climbing the mountain to give up his promised son.

I had already committed to do what He asked, so I couldn't say "no" now—even though part of me wanted to! Even so, I had more faith in His plan, than mine. So, reluctantly and sincerely I replied, "Yes, I'll do anything you ask." He then flashed a vision across my mind: A brand new . . .

camper. Which was the last thing I wanted to move into. I asked Him to confirm this was our next move, by having Andrew suggest it. We had no conversation about it—we were in the middle of church.

Then the pastor takes the stage and has the audacity to start his sermon with, "God wants to stretch your YES," and proceeds to tell the story about a time when God asked Abraham to sacrifice Isaac, the son of the promise. I about hit the floor . . . but as if this wasn't confirmation enough, before service ended Andrew leaned over and whispered, "Do you think God wants us to buy our own camper?" To which I laughed and replied, "Yes, yes I do." We knew what God wanted us to do, and we went for it. It wasn't our choice but we trusted His. We bought a camper within three days, no problems with the bank, every door was opened and it went as smooth as butter. But y'all know what happened next, within a few months the tree disaster occurred.

So we listened to God, we stepped out in faith and followed His plan, and within months our life was in utter disarray. But in the midst of chaos I got the revelation of the gospel of peace. I discovered the promise of peace was included in the good news and Jesus came and sacrificed Himself so I could operate in it supernaturally.

I don't know if I would have learned it any other way. God's ways and plans are truly higher than ours. I surely didn't think buying a camper, seeing it wrecked before our eyes—leaving us homeless, was how I'd discover a peace that never fades, but God did.

To wrap this all up with a pretty bow, within a month we found our dream land in our dream location. We inquired of the Lord, *Do we go back and buy another camper, or what's the plan?* God wanted us to trust Him and move forward to offer on the property, and we did this by faith in His direction, because we knew what the bank had said before. We were truly having to walk by faith, not sight . . . believing the report of the Lord not the report of the bank! Our offer was accepted instantly! Then we reached out to the bank and they miraculously approved our land, no problems. What was happening?! Six months prior it was an absolute, no way this is happening. The only thing that changed in our life was the camper fiasco, which turned out to be what got us the land!

On paper, it looked as though we had purchased an 80,000 dollar camper, and paid it off in three months. What they didn't know was: the insurance paid it off! Haha! This made our credit look awesome.

Suddenly banks were approving us—because apparently we pay off lots of debt fast. God knows what He is doing and we have to trust even if and especially when we don't understand!

Do you see how faith led us here? Walking by faith in what God told us to do got us across the finish line in the most unusual way. I could never have planned this! The Lord didn't want us to give up the farm He promised, He was just testing our faith! When His plan didn't line up with ours, when what we saw didn't match what He said, who would we trust? His word or our way? Faith in God moved our mountain and it will do the same for you! Let's dive into the shield of faith and learn how to trust God more than anything else and overcome any obstacle the enemy throws our way!

— Amber

SHEILD OF FAITH

Scan for session ten video

SESSION TEN NOTES:

DAY ONE
Jesus is the shield!

Isn't it completely amazing how each part of the armor of God aligns flawlessly and relies on the other pieces to work in perfect tandem?! Did ya notice how we are talking through the shield of faith last, even though it is listed earlier in the gear? Well this is strategic, because we want to take this week to show how to use the shield of faith to block every attack, now that we're aware of what all the other pieces mean.

You know us well enough by now that we love looking up the Greek and Hebrew meanings of words in scripture, and faith is no different.

RESEARCH MORE

Faith is the Greek word *pistis*: faith, faithfulness, belief, trust, confidence, fidelity [16]

We rolled out this study with a pretty bold statement. The armor of God is really Jesus, and in this study we've been learning how to rest in Him and what He has done for us—this is how we are truly Armored Up, and the shield of faith is no different! The shield is Jesus, and our faith comes from Him. We'll show ya, look up the following scriptures and fill in the missing words.

> THE _____ IS MY STRENGTH AND MY _____; MY HEART _____ IN HIM, AND I AM HELPED. THEREFORE MY HEART REJOICES, AND I GIVE THANKS TO HIM WITH MY SONG.
> PSALM 28:7 NIV

Who is our shield?

The LORD always means Jesus, because He is the King of kings and LORD of lords (Revelation 19:16), He is the LORD Jesus Christ, so even when we see the "LORD" in the Old Testament it is always speaking of our Savior. Notice in the verse it doesn't say: The LORD gives me a shield, no! It says "The LORD is my shield!"

Anyone else think this is Amazing?!

Okay, now look at this in reference to faith.

> JESUS, THE _____ AND _____ OF OUR _____, WHO FOR THE JOY THAT WAS SET BEFORE HIM ENDURED THE CROSS, DESPISING THE SHAME, AND IS SEATED AT THE RIGHT HAND OF THE THRONE OF GOD.
> HEBREWS 12:2 ESV

In relation to our faith Jesus is the:

1.

2.

RESEARCH MORE

Founder is the Greek word: *archégos*: founder, leader, originator, author, prince [17]

Pair the Greek definition with the verse, Jesus is the prince of our faith (kinda like He's the prince of our peace, right?). He is the leader of our faith, the originator and the author of it. He is where we get our faith from! The shield of faith is again not about us, but Him! Surprise, surprise.

RESEARCH MORE

We can't forget about perfecter though. This is the Greek word *teleiótés*: a perfecter, a completer, finisher [18]

Jesus completes our faith. He perfects it. Wow, pressure off! Something shifted when we realized faith is what Jesus does in us and is actually a gift and fruit of the Holy Spirit. It is not something we muster up on our own, it's the very strength of Jesus actively working through us and it grows as we exercise it.

> BUT THE FRUIT OF THE _____ IS LOVE, JOY, PEACE, FORBEARANCE, KINDNESS, GOODNESS, _____, GENTLENESS AND SELF-CONTROL. AGAINST SUCH THINGS THERE IS NO LAW.
> GALATIANS 5:22-23 NIV

We bet you can guess the Greek word used for faithfulness here. That is right, pistis. So really that scripture could read one fruit of the Spirit is faith. Again, as we walk in closer relationships with the Spirit our faith develops! How incredible to comprehend that Jesus is our shield of faith! This is a pretty great defense, actually the best! Amazing!!

We get both our protection and faith from Him. Similar to every other piece of the armor—we are righteous because Jesus is righteous, we experience salvation and deliverance because He saved us and is our Deliverer, we have peace because He is our Prince of Peace and gave us His peace, we have truth because He is the truth—so it is the same with faith: We are full of faith because He is faithful!

Journaling

SECRET PLACE Training

Do you ever wonder if you have "enough" faith?

How did the study today encourage you?

Say a prayer and release this feeling of needing to have "more faith" into the hands of Jesus, the prince and leader of your faith. Instead, ask Him to perfect and complete your faith, as the Word says.

DAY TWO
believe in His faithfulness

"*Some boast about their faithfulness and good works. I choose to boast on the faithfulness of God and His good work. He Already Did it!*" Marol Vallejo, a friend of ours, posted this quote THE DAY we were writing the devotional content for the week of faith! Isn't God's timing SO perfect? The truth is we grow in our ability to use the shield of faith, when we trust in God's faithfulness. Our focus needs to be on how faithful our God is! We'll show you how, let's take a look at "Father Abraham" one more time. He is often called the 'father of faith' in Christianity, because of his great—you guessed it—faith. Look up the following scriptures (breifly recounting the story of Abraham believing God for a son, after they were physically too old for this to happen) and fill in the blanks. We're about to discover the secret of great faith!

THAT IS WHY IT DEPENDS ON _____, IN ORDER THAT THE PROMISE MAY REST ON GRACE AND BE GUARANTEED TO ALL HIS OFFSPRING—NOT ONLY TO THE ADHERENT OF THE LAW BUT ALSO TO THE ONE WHO …

_____ OF ABRAHAM, WHO IS THE FATHER OF US ALL, AS IT IS WRITTEN, "I HAVE MADE YOU THE FATHER OF MANY NATIONS"—IN THE PRESENCE OF THE GOD IN WHOM HE BELIEVED, WHO GIVES LIFE TO THE DEAD AND CALLS INTO EXISTENCE THE THINGS THAT DO NOT EXIST. IN HOPE HE BELIEVED AGAINST HOPE, THAT HE SHOULD BECOME THE FATHER OF MANY NATIONS, AS HE HAD BEEN TOLD, "SO SHALL YOUR OFFSPRING BE." HE DID NOT WEAKEN IN _____ WHEN HE CONSIDERED HIS OWN BODY, WHICH WAS AS GOOD AS DEAD (SINCE HE WAS ABOUT A HUNDRED YEARS OLD), OR WHEN HE CONSIDERED THE BARRENNESS OF SARAH'S WOMB. NO _____ MADE HIM WAVER CONCERNING THE PROMISE OF GOD, BUT HE GREW STRONG IN HIS _____ AS HE GAVE GLORY TO GOD, FULLY _____ THAT _____ TO DO WHAT HE HAD _____.

ROMANS 4:16-21 ESV

> SO HERE WE SEE GOD'S PROMISE OF GRACE RESTS ON ANY WHO HAVE THE _____ OF ABRAHAM. NOT ONLY THAT, BUT AT THE END WE SEE WHY ABRAHAM HAD UNSHAKEABLE FAITH. IT SAYS:
> HE WAS FULLY _____, THAT GOD WAS _____ TO DO WHAT HE PROMISED!

He had faith because he believed in the God who had made him the promise. His faith grew because he believed that God could and would do it.

The secret of great faith is believing in God's faithfulness and God's ability, not ours.

Do you know why Abraham was considered right with God? It sure wasn't His behavior, he slept with his servant and lied on multiple occasions, but it wasn't obedience that declared Abraham righteous, look at this:

> IF HIS GOOD DEEDS HAD MADE HIM ACCEPTABLE TO GOD, HE WOULD HAVE HAD SOMETHING TO BOAST ABOUT. BUT THAT WAS NOT GOD'S WAY. FOR THE SCRIPTURES TELL US, ABRAHAM _____ GOD, AND GOD COUNTED HIM AS _____ BECAUSE . . . OF HIS _____.
> ROMANS 4:2-3 NLT

Circle the correct answer:

- Abraham believed/doubted God.
- God counted him sinner/righteous.
- He was righteous based on faith/action.

Do you see how Abraham is our father in the faith? He was the first person ever considered right with God by faith?! We realize perhaps we've soundend like a broken record but it is SO important to hear it over and over until it transfers from our heads to our heart: We are righteous by faith. Abraham was right with God because he believed God!!! Not because he was perfect. He believed God was able to do everything He said, and that caused him to be a person of great faith and it has the same effect on us! As we feed on God's faithfulness—by recounting all the times He has come through for us, reading the stories throughout the Bible, and hearing the message of Christ—our faith begins to rise! Trust in the faithfulness of the LORD and you'll find your shield and heart of faith is growing stronger. You will hold that shield of faith with confidence because you are fully trusting the God who spoke the Word will complete it!

SECRET PLACE Training

One way to build your faith is to revisit the ways that God has been faithful in your own life. Grab a notebook and take inventory on the different situations or seasons in your life in which God has been faithful to you. Did He open a door that no one else could have? Did He provide for your needs time and time again? Did He heal you or a loved one from physical or emotional pain? List a few instances of the faithfulness of God in your life.

After recounting the past, look at your current circumstances. Is there any area of life you need Him to come through again? List each one. Then, declare *"Father you were faithful before and I know you will be faithful now! I trust in Your faithfulness!"*

Now, take some time in prayer thanking the LORD for being so faithful in your life. Declare the faithfulness of God! Praise Him! Two great songs to help fill the air with faith are "God of Abraham" and "Faithful Now," by Vertical Worship.
.

Journaling

DAY THREE
the shield and the sword

Jesus is our shield, and our faith grows as we trust in God's faithfulness, so how do we use the shield to fight off the flaming arrows of the enemy? You use the shield with the sword. The enemy's attack is predictable. He is going to use our situations to make us question the Word. He is going to whisper lies that make us question our identity. He will use any means possible, hoping we don't know what scripture says about it. We saw back in the sword of the Spirit week what Jesus did when the enemy came His way . . . He replied with the Word, every time. Jesus put more trust in what His Father had said than the lie or temptation the devil was dangling, and so must we! Let's look at our theme scripture for this piece of the armor:

> IN ALL CIRCUMSTANCES
> _____ THE SHIELD OF
> _____, WITH WHICH
> YOU _____ EXTINGUISH
> _____ THE FLAMING DARTS
> OF THE EVIL ONE.
> EPHESIANS 6:16 ESV

Circle the correct answer:

- With the shield of faith you can't/can extinguish enemy attacks.

- With your spiritual shield lifted up you can put out some/all of the flaming darts of the evil one.

RESEARCH MORE

The Greek word for take up is *analambanó*: to take up, raise, pick up, take on board, carry off, lead away [19]

Utilizing the shield of faith requires us to exercise it, we've got to pick it up—that is why both the sword and shield are in our hands! But how is this done practically? Just like we have to lift a weight for it to build our muscle, we too, must lift up our shield by believing and speaking the Word over every single attack to see it be effective. We might have our shield, but are we using it?! Y'all may know the following, very famous Revelation scripture, fill in those blanks, friends.

> THEY TRIUMPHED OVER HIM BY THE _____ AND BY THE _____ OF THEIR _____; THEY DID NOT LOVE THEIR LIVES SO MUCH AS TO SHRINK FROM DEATH.
> REVELATION 12:11 NIV

What two things caused the believers to triumph:

1.

2.

Just like the shield and the sword work together, so triumph over the flaming arrows comes by knowing what Jesus' blood accomplished for us and raising our voice. God's Word and promises are our protection, it's time to believe it! Here's how it works. Let's say the enemy tries to convince you that no one loves you. Then you have a choice, to either believe that thought, or pick up your shield and say "No, I'm not going to believe that, I'm going to put my faith in what God's Word says! I know that in Ephesians 1:4 (NLT) the Bible says:

> EVEN BEFORE HE MADE THE WORLD, GOD _____ US & CHOSE US _____ TO BE HOLY AND WITHOUT FAULT IN HIS EYES.
> EPHESIANS 1:4

So even though I might feel left out or feel unloved at the moment, I know that's not true! God loves me and I believe what He said!"

The shield went up as we "believed" the Word, the sword came out as we "spoke" the Word. Shield up. Sword used. Flaming arrow extinguished. Do you see how the shield works with the sword? You lift up the shield by choosing to put more faith in what His Word says, than what you are experiencing. You believe it AND you speak it. This is how we change the game.

Now the devil will attack every piece of your armor, make no mistake. He'll come after the truth—He always has, don't we remember what He said to Eve in the garden, "Did God really say . . . ?" To which we will reply: "Yes! Yes He did and here is where!" Pull out the Bible, and quote a verse which addresses the lie! Believe in the Word and keep it on your lips!

The enemy will also come for your salvation, making you question, *Am I even saved?* But all we have to do is declare what the Word says. Do you put more faith in the scripture and what Jesus did or in what you did? Declare with boldness, "I am saved because the Word says in Romans 10:13 . . .

> FOR 'EVERYONE WHO _____ ON THE NAME OF THE LORD WILL BE _____.
> ROMANS 10:13 ESV

And guess who I call on as LORD? Jesus. So yes, I am saved. I'm not perfect, but I am covered!"

He will absolutely make you think you aren't righteous. He loves to do this, and will use anyone, anywhere to make you think you've done something and now you aren't right with God, but just lift that shield of faith in Jesus and speak out scripture. "Well guess what, I'm not righteous because of my behavior!! I never have been. I am right with God because of what Jesus did for me, because in Romans 9:30 it says:

> EVEN THOUGH THE GENTILES WERE NOT TRYING TO FOLLOW GOD'S STANDARDS, THEY WERE MADE _____. AND IT WAS BY _____ THAT THIS TOOK PLACE.
> ROMANS 9:30 NLT

Looks like my faith in Christ makes me right with God, not my works, so that is a lie."

Every piece of the armor depends on faith and specifically it hinges on our faith in Christ.

- We have <u>faith</u> that the Word of God is the **truth** and the Word made flesh is Jesus.
- We are **saved** by grace through <u>faith</u> in Christ.
- We are made **righteous** by <u>faith</u> in Jesus.
- We have **peace** with God because of our <u>faith</u> in the LORD.
- We have <u>faith</u> that when we lift our **sword**—using our lips to speak God's Word, that something shifts because we have the authority of Christ!

What is one piece of the armor where you notice the enemy attacks most?

Look through the Word and find a scripture to put faith in and to declare next time those fiery arrows come. Watch them get completely extinguished by using the shield of faith with the sword of the Spirit. Write your scripture below:

Faith in God's Word will protect us, everytime! When we see those enemy arrows coming our way, we must remember it is Jesus and His Word that is our protection—but we must raise our shield and use it to thwart the attacks!

SECRET PLACE Training

Sink into these truths, but also, let these truths sink into you. When the enemy comes, we must use what we've learned, use the word of God and put our faith in every word that He's given us. Let's use every piece of this armor He's given us and take down the enemy!

Look up Psalm 91:4 and write it out.

Notice it says His promises are your armor and protection. You are Armored Up when you know what His Word says and what God has promised you. Ask your Heavenly Father to highlight past ways the enemy has attacked you, and give you verses for every single area. This is how we learn to protect ourselves and prepare for war. We don't wait until the attack comes to learn how to fight, we train before it comes and learn how to dismantle it with scripture!

DAY FOUR
living by faith

When you truly have faith in something, it moves you to action. Like when Peter saw Jesus walking on water—after hearing his Savior say, "Come," Peter got out of the boat and walked on water . . . He had faith and it moved him from on the boat to on the waves (see Matthew 14:25-29). If Peter did not have faith in Jesus' word and ability, he would have not left the boat. Let's look at another scripture that illustrates this perfectly, look it up and complete the verse.

> IN THE SAME WAY, _____ BY ITSELF, IF IT IS NOT ACCOMPANIED BY _____, IS DEAD.
> JAMES 2:17 NIV

Faith without an action is?

When we believe in something, our actions back it up. Now, does this scripture contradict everything that we just talked about? No! Not at all. Consider this: what good is a shield of faith if you are not gonna raise it? If you're not working the armor . . . the armor is not going to work for you.

The work we believe the book of James is talking about is like working out our salvation—we have to do some things in order to grow and become more like Jesus. We have to put on our helmet of salvation and renew our minds by being in the Word. We fasten our belt of truth when we intentionally set aside time to learn the scriptures! We wear our breastplate of righteousness when we understand our identity and commit to memory the Bible verses about God's righteousness by faith! We have to put in the work to experience the peace and wholeness of the gospel. Faith isn't passive, it is active. If we believe it, we're going to study to show ourselves approved! We put the armor on, fully clothed in Christ and learn to live in Him when we have faith in everything the Word says concerning each piece. We must work the tools if we want to get the results!

We have to do our part but it's not about having faith in our part, but keeping our faith in Jesus.

Armor Up

Look up Hebrews eleven, and fill in the missing words below.

> NOW _____ IS _____ IN WHAT WE HOPE FOR AND _____ ABOUT WHAT WE _____.
> HEBREWS 11:1 NIV

Faith is described with what two words:

C

A

When we live by faith, we have confidence in what God has said more than what we see. This is what it means to walk by faith not by sight! Like Abraham, we live fully assured that what God has said is even more true than our reality!

There are days when we may feel we've messed up so bad, there is absolutely no way we could still be counted righteous. What we see is our ungodly behavior. We're painfully aware of our humanity. But this is the moment we need to exercise our faith most! We lift our shield of faith by declaring what the Bible says about our righteousness. You may see yourself and how you fall short, but what matters is not what you see, but what you have faith in.

> FOR WHAT DOES THE SCRIPTURE SAY? "ABRAHAM _____ GOD, AND IT WAS COUNTED TO HIM AS _____." NOW TO THE ONE WHO WORKS, HIS WAGES ARE NOT COUNTED AS A GIFT BUT AS HIS DUE. AND TO THE ONE WHO DOES NOT WORK BUT _____ IN HIM WHO _____ THE _____, HIS _____ IS COUNTED AS _____...
> ROMANS 4:3-5 ESV

We're going to talk about a few things here. First, what caused Abraham to be counted righteous?

So our belief is a big deal, bigger than we even think! Next, we need to look at the word justify/justified. We see this a lot in the Bible and it's kind of a churchy word. While we've heard it often, we may not fully comprehend the implications of it, the Greek definition clears it right up, and we think you're going to LOVE it!

The Greek word for justify is *dikaioó*: **to show to be righteous, declare righteous, made righteous, acquit, regard as righteous**[20]

Anytime you see the word justified in the Bible you can swap it out for "declared righteous"—with this definition in mind, let's look back at the verse! We'll paraphrase: To the one who doesn't earn it, but believes that God declares the ungodly righteous and this righteous standing is based on their faith! Their what? FAITH. When we understand this, the shield of faith activates! On those days you feel unworthy, ungodly, not good enough, you can quote this! It is in that very moment we must have faith in what God's Word says above what we see even about ourselves! "Well I don't have to be good enough, Jesus was, and I am hidden in Him!" It is God who declares me righteous because of my faith in His Son. When we get this, we're shielded from the wrong thinking about our identity. Our actions line up with our identity. When we understand we're declared righteous we start acting that way!

Wearing the armor of God is ultimately realizing: We're never again going to be "out" of Christ, and this brings us peace and protection from lies. Look at this scripture, where Jesus highlights this, fill in the blanks:

> "REMAIN IN _____, AS I ALSO REMAIN IN _____. NO BRANCH CAN BEAR FRUIT BY . . . ITSELF; IT MUST _____ IN THE VINE. NEITHER CAN YOU BEAR FRUIT UNLESS YOU _____."
> JOHN 15:4 NIV

Who does Jesus tell us to remain in?

Just like He always remains in?

Jesus doesn't peace out every time we don't act right. He actually said He would NEVER leave us or forsake us. It is the same for us, guys. He essentially says, "Just like I am remaining in you, you've got to understand you are remaining in me. You don't leave. This is a forever thing and once you grasp this, you are going to produce SO much fruit!!"

This study is about grasping this: WE ARE IN CHRIST! The armor is Jesus, we're in Him—we just have to believe it! Remember we started today with: Faith moves you to action? If we have faith that we are in Christ, we're going to start acting like it.

If we believe the Savior of the world is in us and His words have power, then that means our words have power, and we're going to use them to shift the atmosphere, everywhere we go.

If we see the Word of God as our most potent weapon, knowing as we speak it angels literally watch to perform it (Psalm 103:20), then we're going to be speaking out Bible verses all the time.

Using the shield of faith is about living a lifestyle of faith built on believing what the Bible says and doing something about it! When an attack comes we aren't going to stand for it. We know better—we know what the Word says and we won't tolerate lies anymore! Let us be known as people who LIVE BY FAITH! Raise those shields, nullify the attacks, and let's advance, fully Armored Up to take back ALL the ground!

SECRET PLACE Training

Do you believe you are always and forever hidden in Christ, or do you tend to think you don't always "remain" in Him?

Look up Galatians 2:20 and write it below.

We now live our life by what, and in Who?

Wearing the armor of God is about living a life of faith in Jesus! He loves us, He died for us to walk in victory! Pray and ask the Lord to sink this truth into you, so you can sink fully into His armor! *Father, if there is any part of this I am not understanding, will you make it plain? Reveal it to me by the power of your Holy Spirit who is my teacher! Help me learn what it truly means to live in Christ and to live by faith in Him, not myself! Help me live Armored Up!*

Journaling

FINAL WORD

After taking a deep dive into each piece of the armor of God, and researching other places in the Word where it is mentioned, we hope your understanding of what God has given you to walk in is crystal clear. God gave us His best as our protection and weapon—Jesus His very own Son! We need to live each and every day with an awareness of being clothed in Christ, covered by Him, hidden within our Savior.

We are one with Jesus! We are righteous because He is. We have peace because He does. We are faithful because of His faith in us. We are filled with truth because He is the Truth. We are saved because He is the rock of our salvation! We have the sword of spirit because He is the Word and He is our sword! When people say it's all about Jesus—friends, it literally is!

Knowing who He is, and who we are in Him causes us to enter the rest of God. We have eternal peace, but this doesn't mean we don't engage in warfare, on the contrary, we now know people aren't our enemy. We are aware of the ways the devil attacks, and we don't let him steal our peace! We are Armored Up and we stay at rest while we walk in our authority to resist the devil and he will flee. Engaging in warfare doesn't mean we lose our peace. No, now we operate in it and we put to flight anything that threatens it. But we don't stop there, knowing who we are and Whose we are, we stand firm and advance, taking back ground the enemy has stolen, declaring:

Overwhelming victory is ours through Christ, who loved us!
Romans 8:37 NLT

The world has always been entrusted to mankind, now let's take it back!

NOTES

1. Bible Hub. Accessed August 16, 2023. https://biblehub.com/greek/1746.htm.

2. Bible Hub. Accessed August 16, 2023. https://biblehub.com/greek/37.htm.

3. Google. Accessed August 16, 2023. Google search results. Identity.

4. Bible Hub. Accessed August 16, 2023. https://biblehub.com/greek/544.htm

5. Bible Hub. Accessed August 16, 2023. https://biblehub.com/greek/932.htm.

6. Bible Hub. Accessed August 16, 2023. https://biblehub.com/greek/1343.htm.

7. Bible Hub. Accessed August 16, 2023. https://biblehub.com/greek/3341.htm.

8. Merriam Webster Dictionary. Accessed August 16, 2023. https://www.merriam-webster.com/dictionary/established.

9. Bible Hub. Accessed August 16, 2023. https://biblehub.com/greek/4598.htm.

10. Bible Hub. Accessed August 16, 2023. https://biblehub.com/hebrew/7965.htm.

11. Bible Hub. Accessed August 16, 2023. https://biblehub.com/hebrew/4951.htm.

12. Bible Hub. Accessed August 16, 2023. https://biblehub.com/greek/1515.htm.

13. Bible Hub. Accessed August 16, 2023. https://biblehub.com/greek/3650.htm.

14. Bible Hub. Accessed August 16, 2023. https://biblehub.com/greek/4991.htm.

15. Bible Hub. Accessed August 18, 2023. https://biblehub.com/greek/4151.htm.

16. Bible Hub. Accessed August 16, 2023. https://biblehub.com/greek/4102.htm.

17. Bible Hub. Accessed August 16, 2023. https://biblehub.com/greek/747.htm.

18. Bible Hub. Accessed October 2, 2023. https://biblehub.com/greek/5051.htm.

19. Bible Hub. Accessed August 16, 2023. https://biblehub.com/greek/353.htm.

20. Bible Hub. Accessed August 16, 2023. https://biblehub.com/greek/1344.htm.

ABOUT THE AUTHORS

Amber Olafsson is first and foremost a daughter of the Most High and lover of Jesus. She wears many hats including wife, mom, author, Kingdom entrepreneur, ministry leader, and good news spreader. Amber has a passion to see people encounter God and watch their lives be set ablaze with His holy fire. She and her husband co-founded United House Ministries and United House Worship. Together, they own Allegiance Coffee, a craft coffee shop company that employs and empowers individuals with disabilities and creates opportunities for people to own their own businesses. Amber is also the owner of the Christian publication company United House Publishing and founder of The Light Conference. The Olafssons live with their three energetic, world-changing kiddos, and her ever-growing flock of chickens and livestock guardian dog, Lila, in North Carolina. When she is not relaxing on the back patio with a good book and a hot cup of coffee, she enjoys writing, helping others tell their stories, taking trips with her family, and spending time at the feet of Jesus. Check out her recent book: *I'll Say Yes* online, and to learn more about her day-to-day life follow her on Instagram @amberolafsson

Dianne Wyper is many things to many people, but to all, she is the Jesus-loving girl next door. As an author and speaker, Dianne longs to help women reclaim their true identity. She believes that by equipping women in truth and encouraging them in love, she may see the women of God take their place and step into their calling, becoming all they were created to be. As a wife, mother, and friend, Dianne likes to keep her home in Michigan full of people. She loves to cultivate God's greatness in each heart that comes through her home by using her creativity and warm gatherings to inspire honest conversation about Jesus. As a self-proclaimed atmosphere junkie, she also believes firmly in plenty of good coffee, great food, and laughter. When Dianne isn't spending time with her husband and two kiddos, or diving into a new project or book, you can find her encouraging others through one of her many other outlets. Get to know Dianne by checking out her latest book, *Shattered*, and following her on Instagram @diannewyper